'We are in need of scholars who can combine se.
analysis with professional practice and engaged
Ryder is such a researcher. His excellent *Sites of F*
wide audience.'

**Professor Miklos Hadas, Corvinus University Budapest**


'Ryder's research carries important lessons. He has torn up the rule book
of conventional academic studies, and in the process created a work
of stunning attractiveness, deep insight and great originality, using the
methods of ethnography, participant observation and direct interaction.'

**Dr Marius Taba, Educationalist and Roma community campaigner**

# Sites of Resistance

*I dedicate this volume to my political and academic mentors: Thomas Acton, Susan Alexander, Rodney Bickerstaffe, Sarah Cemlyn, Cllr Rosemary Sales, the late Ann Bagehot, Charlie Smith and Len Smith, and finally to my partner Henrietta and son Arthur.*

# Sites of Resistance

Gypsies, Roma and Travellers in school, the community and the academy

Andrew Ryder

 is an imprint of

First published in 2017 by the UCL Institute of Education Press, University College London, 20 Bedford Way, London WC1H 0AL

www.ucl-ioe-press.com

British Library Cataloguing in Publication Data:
A catalogue record for this publication is available from the British Library

ISBNs
978-1-85856-697-9 (paperback)
978-1-85856-831-7 (PDF eBook)
978-1-85856-832-4 (ePub eBook)
978-1-85856-833-1 (Kindle eBook)

Typeset by Quadrant Infotech (India) Pvt Ltd
Printed by CPI Group (UK) Ltd, Croydon, CR0 4YY
Cover design by emc design. Image by Daniel Jones / Alamy Stock Photo

# Contents

# List of abbreviations

| | |
|---|---|
| COHRE | Centre on Housing Rights and Evictions |
| CRE | Commission for Racial Equality |
| EANRS | European Academic Network on Romani Studies |
| ERI | European Roma Institute |
| ERTF | European Roma Traveller Forum |
| EU | European Union |
| GCSE | General Certificate of Secondary Education |
| GTLRC | Gypsy and Traveller Law Reform Coalition (non-governmental organization) |
| HMI | Her Majesty's Inspector |
| IRU | International Romani Union |
| LGBT | lesbian, gay, bisexual and transgender |
| NGOs | non-governmental organizations |
| Ofsted | Office for Standards in Education |
| OSCE | Organization for Security and Co-operation in Europe |
| RREN | Roma Research and Empowerment Network |
| RSS | regional spatial strategies |
| SEN | special educational needs |
| TES | Traveller Education Services |

# Acknowledgements

I am deeply indebted to Dr Sarah Cemlyn (University of Bristol) and Professor Miklos Hadas (Corvinus University of Budapest) for the invaluable comments I received on the manuscript of this book. I also wish to thank Gillian Klein, PhD, Senior Fellow in Publishing and Publisher of Trentham Books for her guidance and encouragement in producing this book.

# About the author

*Andrew Ryder* is an Associate Professor at the Corvinus University of Budapest and Associate Fellow at the Third Sector Research Centre at the University of Birmingham. Prior to this he was Policy Officer to the Irish Traveller Movement in Britain and the Gypsy and Traveller Law Reform Coalition, and researcher for the All-Party Parliamentary Group for Gypsies, Roma and Travellers.

# Foreword

Research, campaigns and reports have for decades documented the inequalities and injustices experienced by Gypsies, Travellers and, more recently, Roma living in the UK. Most recently, The Traveller Movement's (2016) submission to the Universal Periodic Review of the United Nations Human Rights Council reported on discrimination and poor access to services across the board, a situation exacerbated by government policy, action and inaction, and austerity measures since 2010. It was compiled from a wide range of research and echoed previous studies, such as the Civil Society Monitoring Report on the UK's Roma Strategy led by the National Federation of Gypsy Liaison Groups (Ryder and Cemlyn, 2014) and Council of Europe sponsored reports on health and criminal justice human rights (Greenfields *et al.*, 2015a; 2015b). The Parliamentary Women and Equalities Committee announced an inquiry to 'tackle Gypsy, Roma and Traveller inequalities' in November 2016: the results remain to be seen.

The Traveller Movement submission noted in particular: that 98 per cent of respondents to an online survey reported experiencing discrimination; that severely inadequate planning and provision for suitable accommodation for these groups had worsened with the Conservative Government's restrictive change to planning law concerning the definition of 'Gypsy and Traveller' and the abolition of the local authority duty to undertake specific accommodation needs assessments; that the health status and outcomes for Gypsies and Travellers are significantly lower than any similarly disadvantaged comparator groups in terms of adult and infant mortality, chronic illness and access to services (European Commission, 2014; Greenfields *et al.*, 2015a); that significantly lower educational attainment than any other group (DfE, 2016) remains amid endemic bullying and persistent difficulties of engagement between some schools and the communities; and that the communities are over-represented as offenders in criminal justice systems throughout Europe but significantly under-represented as victims in the system (Greenfields *et al.*, 2015b).

This is the background to this book, which focuses in particular on education, community development and activism, and research philosophy and approaches. It is both a personal and a political account of engagement, education, activism and research with Gypsy and Traveller communities since the 1990s. It delves deeply into the nature and challenges of Gorgios (non-Gypsy/Roma people) working in support of and alongside Gypsies, Roma and Travellers. We were honoured to be asked to write this foreword, having travelled along some similar paths involving practice, activism and research to Dr Ryder's more extensive and pioneering journey, from which we have also learnt much: Felicity Bonel via play work, teaching, coordination of two Traveller Education Services (TES), organizational advocacy and academic studies on identity, and health and well-being; Sarah Cemlyn via welfare rights and community development work through non-governmental organizations (NGOs) and support groups, education liaison work in a TES and collaborative and co-produced research on welfare, education, accommodation and human rights. For each of us, the integration of practice, research and collaborative advocacy for social justice and equality alongside Gypsies, Roma and Travellers has been an important foundation; a model that Ryder's book vividly highlights.

Beginning in the 1960s, slow improvements in education for Gypsies, Roma and Travellers took place, with the gradual development of TES and the appointment of Her Majesty's Inspector (HMI) for Gypsy, Roma and Traveller children from the mid-1970s. However, ongoing cuts to the national TES network since 2011, the lack of an HMI since 2003, and the devolvement of funding to schools have left Gypsy, Roma and Traveller communities without dedicated support within the education system. Their educational position is considered in depth through the case study of Ryder's research in a secondary school and the nearby site in 2002, which provides a nuanced examination of processes of resistance within a particular Gypsy community vis-à-vis their local school.

The Gypsy, Roma and Traveller third sector also has 1960s' roots, with the Gypsy Council's campaign against evictions, a high point being its hosting of the first World Romani Congress in 1971. Education was also an NGO focus in voluntary summer schools, the National Gypsy Education Council and the subsequent breakaway Advisory Council for the Education of Romanies and other Travellers, reflecting a split between competing views of rights to mainstream education versus cultural assimilation. Another high point was diverse groups joining forces in 2002 to form the Gypsy and Traveller Law Reform Coalition (GTLRC), whose campaign for a reinstatement of legislative responsibility to provide or facilitate sites was broadly successful, although the GTLRC ceded to internal tensions and burnout in 2006. Ryder gives us an insider's view of the GTLRC as a social movement. Over time, grassroots groups have grown and folded, and a few larger NGOs have gained an increasing national profile, while the mechanisms for community control have increased. However, overall the Gypsy, Roma and Traveller third sector is small and fragmented, with only about 30 groups, mainly struggling against hostile pressures and lack of resources.

Research is a third recurrent and increasingly insistent theme of Andrew Ryder's life path alongside Gypsy, Roma and Traveller communities, through his PhD studies and co-produced activist research to the establishment of the Roma Research and Empowerment Network in Budapest. Ryder addresses emerging debates about detached elitist academic research versus participatory egalitarian research that validates the standpoint and experience of minorities.

Echoing the traditionally gendered structures of Gypsy, Roma and Traveller communities, the worlds of academia and of activism by and with these communities have, until recently, been similarly gendered. Ryder draws our attention to changes in this respect among Gypsy and Traveller women activists, who within their communities are often deemed to be best equipped to deal with the authorities.

As we write this in the aftermath of the deeply unsettling 2016 US presidential election and the UK's Brexit debate, with societal divisions and grievances generated by profound inequality exploited for troubling political ends, we all face the challenge of being able to listen to each other across wide political gulfs. The current political climate poses possibly unprecedented challenges, with rising racism and intolerance across the Western world. Gypsies and Travellers and, in particular, Roma community members are especially vulnerable in this situation. Moving away from divisions between 'practitioner', 'academic' and 'activist' and creating partnerships between Gypsies, Roma and Travellers and their friends and allies can strengthen and build upon many years of work to promote justice and inclusion. Already, young people from these communities are coming forward as future representatives and leaders.

In this very personal book, Andrew Ryder shows the value of reflective practice in intercultural working and the importance of overtly linking theory and practice. His ability to do this throughout his working life places him in the unusual position of being able to bring this dynamic to bear on his analysis of his subject matter and it makes for both fascinating and enlightening reading. His honesty in exploring the roots of his own interest in liminal communities and intense cultural shifts and tensions means that this book holds also a wider relevance for how to sustain critical citizenship and solidarity across boundaries of identity and belonging in these traumatic political times.

*Felicity Bonel and Sarah Cemlyn*
*Felicity Bonel and Sarah Cemlyn both have a long-standing record of research and educational work with Gypsy, Roma and Traveller communities.*

# Chapter 1

# A pedagogy of hope for Gypsies, Roma and Travellers

## Introduction

This book is about Gypsies, Roma and Travellers and their resistance to oppression. Gypsies, who migrated from India, are first recorded in Britain in the early sixteenth century. Their nomadic traditions brought them into conflict with the Tudor state, which sought to sedentarize travelling communities and exert control over subjects deemed to present a threat to hegemony. This was to be a recurring tension between travelling communities and the state.

Irish Travellers descend from an ancient Celtic (or pre-Celtic) nomadic group and the first reliable record of their presence in Britain dates to the nineteenth century, although they were probably present much earlier. There are also Scottish and other travelling groups. New Travellers, however, are not a distinct ethnic group, but have assumed travelling lifestyles. Gypsies and Irish Travellers traditionally have close-knit family and economic networks, and nomadism – or the possibility of it – remains a strong cultural value in a way that it does not for the mainly sedentary East European Roma. Roma is the term generally used to describe the Romani communities of Central and Eastern Europe because a growing number see the term 'Gypsy' as pejorative, although they belong to the same ethnographic group as British Gypsies. In European documentation and discussions 'Roma' encompasses diverse groups such as Roma, Gypsies and Travellers.

The Roma of Central Eastern Europe have been subject to severe persecution, notably their slaughter during the Holocaust, and to a programme of assimilation during communism. Post-communist society accentuated Roma poverty and marginalization, which in part explains their migration to Britain and other affluent European countries (Ryder *et al.*, 2014). Despite the heterogeneity of Gypsy, Roma and Traveller communities, they all experience racism and marginalization, and this may lead to exploration of what they have in common, and to solidarity.

The book explores how marginalized communities respond to exclusion and mobilize identity as a resource to withstand and challenge injustice through solidarity. Resistance, however, takes various forms and is also reactionary. The book discusses how conservative notions of tradition and identity offer refuge for beleaguered ethnic groups to retreat into, but it is primarily concerned with how identity offers scope for resistance and for fundamental change and betterment.

Key to this process is what Brazilian educator Paolo Freire calls the 'pedagogy of hope' (1994), a belief that the world can be changed. Through reflection on resistance, practice and knowledge, the book considers the power of such hope, but also its fragility, in the spheres of formal education and community activism and resistance.

Education is a key focus, both formal, in schools and the academy, and also emancipatory education and development that might lay down the foundations for effective resistance to injustice by Gypsy, Traveller and Roma communities. Liégeois notes:

> Education increases personal autonomy, providing the tools for adapting to a changing environment and a means of self-defence from the forces of assimilation; it makes it possible to break out of the passive rut of welfarism to play an active role in cultural and political development.
>
> (Liégeois, 1998: 19)

However, traditional educational environments can equally be arenas of oppression for Gypsies, Roma and Travellers, and attempts by them to subvert and resist oppressive practices are described. Questions arise: Is formal education and the acquisition of new cultural capital a priori for the achievement of social justice for Gypsies, Roma and Travellers? Are there inherent dangers of tokenism and assimilation within such strategies? Without education, are they disempowered if they lack the skills to mobilize and are dependent upon outsider leadership?

This book is more theoretical than two other books with which I have been involved, namely Richardson and Ryder (2012) *Gypsies and Travellers: Empowerment and inclusion in British society*, a handbook for practioners, and Ryder *et al.* (2014) *Hearing the Voices of Gypsies, Roma and Travellers: Inclusive community development*, which provides a historical overview of UK Gypsy, Roma and Traveller activism.

The present volume offers insights into social policy and its impact on Gypsies, Roma and Travellers, with particular reference to formal education (cultural capital) and activism and empowerment (critical pedagogy). However, the 'thick description' you will find here is of detailed and intimate life stories. Instead of depersonalized and ahistorical accounts,

I seek to link macro theories with grounded personal biography so that the research is accessible, but I aim also to diminish the authoritative voice in favour of a narrative of people's lives that allows for multiple realities and alternative interpretations (Okely and Callaway, 1992). Although it is auto-ethnographical, a self-narrative, the book finds points of connection with the life stories of others so that its reflexivity does not become solipsistic or narcissistic. The data I present is open to different readings and interpretations.

Like the two earlier volumes, it is influenced by standpoint theory. As a critical researcher I contend that research should be situated in the concerns of marginalized people (Harding, 1991). This brings the researcher closer to valid and meaningful knowledge. Drawing on ethnographic observation conducted in the early 2000s or recounting my first-hand experiences of activism with Gypsy, Roma and Traveller communities allows a platform for their voices. Standpoint theory contends that scientism in research cannot detach itself from the class, culture and race of the researcher, though recognition of their impact through reflexivity reduces the influence of bias (Reinharz, 1997).

## Reflexivity

The ethnographic situation is defined not only by the nature of the observed community, but also by the ethnological tradition of the ethnographer. Once in the field, the research participants' presuppositions also become operative, and the situation turns into complex intercultural mediation and a dynamic and interpersonal experience (Scholte, 1974). Reflexivity can help the researcher make sense of the complex web to which Scholte refers. Notions of the researcher as an impersonal machine are rejected and scientism and positivism are defied once we do not sanitize the 'I' from the narrative (Okely, 1992). Instead, the researcher acknowledges the impact of the different perspectives and life experiences he or she holds and determines how these have shaped his or her research by situating the researcher's perspective through reflexivity. It is important to reflect on the different selves or shades of identity the researcher brings to the research process. In my reflexivity I am also influenced by notions of critical multiculturalism and critical whiteness.

Multiculturalism is often derided as patronizing, tokenistic or divisive, encouraging communities to self-exclude and form spatial and cultural enclaves. However, critical multiculturalism seeks to explore the interplay between race, gender and class and oppressive behaviours and practices (Farrar, 2012). Here is a dialogic and negotiable form of multiculturalism that challenges oppressive outlooks in both majority and minority society; it is a two-way integration, where the identities of all ethnic groups, including white majoritarian society in the UK and Europe, change in response to an overarching national community and sense of identity as it emerges (Modood, 2012). Such conceptions may be the antidote to the assimilationism that emerged post-9/11 (Bourne, 2007). These conceptions of identity and race have guided me in writing this book.

As for critical whiteness, I do not accept the assumption that those who are white, like me, do not have an identity (Delgado and Stefancic, 1997). Imbued with notions of supremacy, white identity is shifting and situational; not long ago, for example, the Irish were considered to be non-white – outside the privileged demarcation of whiteness. Whiteness, contrary to popular opinion, is a heterogeneous identity that reflects different traits of ethnicity, geography and class. Within the dialogic frame of Modood's 'two-way integration', creating a more critical appreciation of white identity may be a key step towards eradicating the racism that white identity and its manipulation perpetuates (Vajda, 2015). I hope that through my story of working with Gypsy, Roma and Traveller communities I can illustrate the value of cultural interaction and reflection.

I was raised in London's commuter belt. My mother came from a poor working-class family; after the Second World War her father moved from rural labouring to construction work on the housing estates being built in outer London. My grandfather had a serious drinking problem that kept the family in poverty. His relationship with my mother was deeply troubled and left her with a strong desire to distance herself from her humble background, of which she was so ashamed. My father's family ran a small family engineering business where he worked on the lathes, even when he became co-owner with his brother.

The first house I lived in was a council house, but from the 1970s the family business flourished and the family was rapidly propelled up the social ladder, moving to ever bigger houses and more affluent neighbourhoods. By the time I reached my teens, my family was comfortably middle class. As a child, my father had worked in the family business and he continued this tradition with me. During my school holidays I was taken to the factory to clean the machines and carry out simple engineering operations, drilling and cutting up pieces of metal. I did not enjoy the work. I hated the tedium and continually watched the clock, wishing the hours away. Was this how I wanted to spend my working life? The experience convinced me that I did not want to continue in the family business after finishing school but to break away. That the best stratagem seemed to be to get into university only dawned on me after I achieved a pass in only one O level (precursor to the General Certificate of Secondary Education (GCSE) taken at the age of 16) and was offered the option to go into the family business. Swift and successful O level retakes and top-grade A levels earned me a university place.

I was the first in my family to go to university and my success surprised some, not least myself. At primary school I was held by staff to have serious attention and behavioural disorders; one of my teachers insisted I be sent to a special school. My parents resisted formal assessments and argued, rightly, that there was a personality clash between me and that teacher. Maybe I recognized that the teacher held a deficit-treatment model of what we now call neurodivergence – how greatly human brains and minds differ. I realized from an early age that I was different but sensed also the hostility and prejudice that such difference could arouse and learnt to try to disguise that difference.

Through the formal assessment of my son as neuorodivergent/autistic I have come to embrace the paradigm that recognizes neurodiversity as a natural and valuable form of human difference and rejects the idea that there is but one 'normal' or 'healthy' type of brain or mind. Majoritarian and mainstream contention of one 'correct' style of neurocognitive functioning is a cultural construct, as prejudiced a notion as the idea of one race or gender being superior to another. The neurodiversity paradigm contends that differences such as autism are the result of normal, natural variation in the human genome and thus should not be pathologized but instead accommodated and where needed supported to function in a world dominated by certain kinds of mind. My history of conflict with authority and my feeling of being an outsider attracted me to movements and groups that were oppositional to the mainstream.

So it was that after a late academic flowering, I found myself at university in Wales feeling utterly disorientated and experiencing severe culture shock. My disorientation together with my inclination for oppositionality prompted an interest in radical Labour politics, a commitment accentuated by Margaret Thatcher's neo-liberal Conservative Government, which was embroiled in the miners' strike of 1984/5. This coincided with my final year of A levels and first year at university. I became heavily involved in Labour Party activism and before starting university I joined Militant, a small cadre of Trotskyite entryists working within the Labour Party. This cultist group attracted me because of the simple solution to the ills of the world it presented. Militant had a sense of immediacy and action – attributes that appealed to a restless young person like me, who wanted to change the world now.

I arrived at university with instructions from Militant to take my time settling in and becoming established in the university Labour Club. The plan was to build a network of friends and gradually raise the profile of Militant until we gained control of the student Labour Club. I managed these tasks well in my first year but Militant became frustrated with me because I deviated from their instructions. The Labour Club contained a variety of activists and although some were interested in Trotskyism, I believed that few were willing to commit fully. Even my own interest waned. I was tired of Militant's hectoring, especially on the occasions I met national contacts, when I wanted to be free to think for myself. The politics of the other students in the club began to influence me, particularly the peace movement and the use of non-violent direct action, but what excited me was socialism of a freer-thinking kind.

Because of my activism in the peace movement in 1985, when I was 19, I was involved in protests against Carmarthen District Council in Wales. The council sought to construct a nuclear bunker but suffered serious construction delays and security costs, thanks to the demonstrations and protests we orchestrated (Parry, 2005). As a consequence of these protests, 17 of us were legally charged with tortious conspiracy and threatened with a bill of £300,000 to cover the costs incurred by the local authority as a result of the protests. I felt I had my back to the wall and the legal charge hung over me for several years, although it was eventually dropped by the local authority. On several levels, socially, culturally and politically, I had experienced the stigma but also the liberation of being an outsider, and this may have given me some empathy for Gypsy, Roma and Traveller communities in my later community activism. After this legal case, I became more involved in mainstream activism, and during postgraduate study served as chairperson of the Constituency Labour Party and as a member of the Executive of the Welsh Labour Party.

Within Labour Party structures outside the university, I was involved with a wide range of people: schoolteachers, nurses, postmen, coalminers, professors... all with disparate views on Labourism. The fraternity I felt in these interactions and the wealth of experience of members I could learn from convinced me that trust and strong networks are the lifeblood of social movements and they inform the activism I strive to develop and maintain in my community work. When trust appears to be lacking, I tend to ask questions of, and even distance myself from, campaigning that seems to be devoid of real networks but has instead become hierarchical and professionalized.

My connection with Gypsies and Travellers has been a long one but it has changed with time. My interaction has been centred on a wide range of roles, such as schoolteacher, researcher, activist and friend. The first formal role I assumed was far from positive. I started my working life in 1990, as a schoolteacher in a school operating in what the Department of Education classified as 'challenging circumstances'. The school was in a poor neighbourhood; academic achievement was poor. Many of the students were housed Gypsies who were disaffected from school. As an inexperienced teacher, I chose to blame such disaffection on antisocial behaviour or poor parenting, rather than on my failings as a teacher or failings of the school. I had been a member of the Labour Party since my teens but it took some time for my egalitarian principles to combine with my experience and maturity as a teacher to develop a more sympathetic understanding of the causes of student alienation.

In 1998, while working for the British Council in Budapest, I embarked on an MA in education by distance learning and centred my research on the educational experiences of Hungarian Roma and later Portuguese Gypsies. My research was rather formalized: I observed students in class but did not interact with them informally. Neither was I involved in campaigning: as a member of the diplomatic service I was precluded from such activity in countries where I was posted. In 2001, I embarked upon full-time PhD studies, adopting a participant observer approach by taking on the role of classroom assistant in several schools. I was also a youth worker on Traveller sites. I resolved to become involved in campaigning at a national level outside the research, in an attempt to fuse ethnography with critical research. This approach afforded me deeper understanding of my research participants and enabled me to link my observations with wider trends and processes in society and governmental policy.

However, I deferred my research to take up a full-time campaign role in Gypsy and Traveller civil society. There was a period of intense political activity between 2003 and 2008, marked by a New Labour Government that began belatedly to consider measures to address Gypsy and Traveller accommodation. This aroused intense opposition from the Conservatives and the tabloid press. This book relates some of what happened.

In 2010 I decided to try to fuse research and activism through an interest in participatory research and took an academic post at the Corvinus University in Budapest. This coincided with a movement towards a paradigm shift in Roma knowledge production, precipitating a bitter clash between positivist and critical researchers. Research can be 'on', 'for' or 'with' the researched (Blaikie, 1995). I am not alone in identifying a long tradition of research 'on' Roma communities (Ryder, 2015c). Since the start of academic interest in Roma communities in the eighteenth century, academia adopted hierarchical research approaches and promoted scientific and cultural racism, thus giving credence to policies of genocide and assimilation. Scholars in the field of Romani studies imbued with scientism have been labelled as 'Gypsylorists' (Mayall, 2004), and they clashed with critically orientated researchers over issues related to the validity, objectivity and authenticity of their respective research approaches. These competing visions epitomize the ivory-tower aloofness and elitism of academia in contrast to the realities of life and the need for solutions to problems lived (Roll-Hansen, 2009). This book offers insights into this critical period of contestation.

It is this kaleidoscope of life experiences and standpoints that has moulded the nature of the inquiry described in this book. *Sites of Resistance* is not an autobiography: my experiences are only referred to where they have some relevance to wider events. The focus is on the ethnogenesis and life strategies of Gypsies and Travellers at the margins. It is informed by 'observation of participation': I observe my own and others' co-participation in various encounters.

## Betwixt and between and performance

As a person labelled 'white' who for most of his life was in a position of relative privilege but who questioned and challenged that state of advantage, I have sought to de-hegemonize my sense of self, a state where according to the critical and feminist thinker Gayatri Chakravorty Spivak one should learn how to occupy the subject position of the other (Landry and MacLean, 1996). Mohanty (1997: xiii) has called for a focus on 'the consolidation of the self rather than the marginalisation of the "Other" as productive in resisting the crafting of white, masculinist, heterosexist, and capitalist citizenship'. Accordingly I strive to understand and embrace alternative world views and life strategies and this has taken me on a journey in a liminal state. The terms 'liminal' and 'liminality' derive from the Latin 'limen' (threshold) – that is, the bottom of a doorway that must be crossed when entering a building. They have been applied to rites of passage, such as coming of age rituals, to help understand the process of change. According to Van Gennep (2010), who was the first to discuss liminality, it is centred on three stages, involving: (1) separation, (2) a liminal period and (3) re-assimilation. The term 'liminal' can be taken outside of its ritual context and applied to societal and cultural experiences of dislocation and search.

In his studies of African tribes, the ethnographer Victor Turner described liminal individuals or entities as 'neither here nor there; they are betwixt and between the positions assigned and arrayed by law, custom, convention, and ceremony' (1995: 95). Turner recognized the wider applicability of the term and the value of analysing those who are 'between'. People in a liminal state are temporarily located within the interstices of social structure, where they are most aware of themselves and most capable of scrutiny and insight. We could, however, take a looser meaning of liminality. One could interpret it as feeling cut off from a stable identity and being in a process of constant change and disorder – a state from which one continually seeks exit. This understanding of the term could then, to a degree, describe my life journey as well as those of the particular groups of Gypsies, Roma and Travellers featured in this book.

The people this book is about displayed aspects of hybridity (Bhabha, 2004), sometimes mirroring the conservative performances of majoritarian society. At the same time, however, especially where tradition was combined with innovation, a counter-hegemonic discourse was evident, challenging the status quo in the manner of Antonio Gramsci's 'organic intellectuals' (see the English translation of Gramsci's *Prison Notebooks*, 1971). Gramsci argued that hegemonic power 'normalizes' the ideology of the ruling class, so that resistance seems absurd. And it follows, therefore, that counter-hegemonic action requires deliberation by intellectuals at the margins who have directly experienced inequality, and not intellectuals from the ruling elite. Gramsci contended that an anti-hegemonic action requires building alliances among those who have broadly shared interests, led by organic rather than traditional intellectuals. This book explores the formation and experiences of 'organic intellectuals' within Gypsy, Roma and Traveller communities.

## Outline of the book: A call to context

The ethnography of my doctoral research forms the basis for the accounts of life on a council Traveller site and families' experiences of school. In contrast, my description of activism is based on memory and direct participation.

Previous research on Gypsy and Traveller school students tends to focus on what happens to them, rather than on what they themselves do or say. In the reports on Gypsies' and Travellers' education, participation and achievement, the subjects appear remote and the human story is rarely told.

So that we can better understand the complexity of the Gypsies' and Travellers' lives, I relate my observations on not only the school environment but also in the homes on Traveller sites. The thick description and detail provided creates a 'call to context' – 'an insistence on the importance of context and the detail of the lived experience of minoritized people as a defence against the colour-blind and sanitized analyses generated by universalistic discourses' (Gillborn, 2008: 30). My research, undertaken 15 years ago, chronicles the experiences of a profoundly marginalized community.

Chapter 2, 'Hegemony and life strategy', sets the policy, historical and cultural context of the book, charting the development of policy towards Gypsies and Travellers after the Second World War, which was driven alternately by localism and statism, with assimilation as the guiding principle.

Chapter 3, 'Cultural trauma, marginalization and resistance', provides a detailed picture of life on a site and the historical, cultural and socio-economic factors that shape identity. It offers detailed insights into the lifeworld of Gypsies and Travellers living on a local authority Traveller site.

Chapter 4, 'School: Resistance and conflict', provides insights into the educational experiences of Gypsies within a school, illustrating how the mismatch between the curriculum and the students' identity and aspirations, along with the school's misconceptions about Gypsies and Travellers, contributed towards these students' exclusion and alienation.

Chapter 5, 'Identity, exclusion and change', explores the nature of conflict between the Gypsies and their peers and the school management more theoretically and reveals how failure to mediate contributes to tensions and polarization within a school and how reactionary and narrow forms of identity can be seen as reactions to exclusion but can often be counterproductive.

Critical theorists have criticized the interpretative approach for its focus on the micro to the detriment of the macro – that by adopting such a narrow approach interpretative research is conservative, as it fails to note structural causes or call for structural change (Hall and Hall, 1996). Some interpretative researchers have responded by trying to develop links between micro and macro analysis. My investigation seeks to evaluate the success of macro policy in raising the inclusion of Gypsies and Travellers in school and society, so it has a critical dimension. Chapter 6, 'Critical pedagogy', describes the struggle of Gypsies and Travellers to secure greater recognition and inclusion in society and their involvement in a social movement. It considers how those at the margins can be empowered through inclusive community development. However, I caution against the dangers of managerialism in activism and stress the value of trust in community mobilization.

Chapter 7, 'Gypsies and Travellers on the front line: Organic intellectuals and strategic ties', looks at Gypsy and Traveller protest and resistance on unauthorized developments – caravan sites with no planning permission – and how community advocates on such sites developed strategic relationships and alliances with a range of outsider actors, and considers the benefits and disadvantages of such ties.

Chapter 8, 'Academic cage fighting, position taking and awakenings within Romani studies', explores the relationship between Gypsies, Roma and Travellers and international Roma civil society and academia. How can they become more connected and relevant to the communities they seek to portray and represent? It is helpful to look beyond the UK to European developments in Roma issues.

The concluding chapter explores the performance of identity and the relevance of education in the recognition, redistribution and representation (Fraser, 2007) of Gypsies, Roma and Travellers in efforts to secure social justice. I hope the book will appeal to a broad audience of students, established academics, practitioners and community members. Even if it cannot possibly satisfy you all, I hope the balance of theory and narrative will be useful to both organic and academic intellectuals as well as practitioners and campaigners, and will contribute to our quest for transformative change.

# Chapter 2

# Hegemony and life strategy

This chapter provides an overview of the historical and cultural context of the experiences of Gypsies and Travellers and of policy development after the Second World War.

## Who are Gypsies and Travellers?

> The electric saw made a sharp searing sound as the blade cut through the protective lagging revealing the prized copper piping. The man steadily cut the pipe into segments. Two young adolescents helped collect the exposed piping and placed it in the bin for copper; at the smelting plant this was the scrap that attracted a high value. A grey cloud of dust enveloped the small scrapyard, dust that emanated from the fire-resistant asbestos lagging of the pipe.
>
> (A recollection of a day in a scrapyard in 1984 –
> we will return to this vignette in Chapter 9)

Self-employment in industries such as scrap metal and recycling, construction and landscaping is a significant feature of the Gypsy and Traveller economy, a form of economic organization that reflects the history and culture of these groups and that has afforded protection, sustenance and cultural reproduction in a world marked by hostility and oppression. But, as the recollection above suggests, life at the margins can involve extreme hardship. The nature and cause of that hardship and the life strategies adopted in response are a recurrent theme in this chapter.

Soon after their arrival in Britain, Gypsies and Travellers found themselves at odds with the establishment. The Tudor and Elizabethan period was marked by moral panics about vagrancy and the introduction of legislation to combat it. The anti-Egyptian laws from the 1550s, which made being a Gypsy a capital offence in itself, constituted a form of ethnic cleansing (Acton, 1974). What were the motivations for such persecutions, which were not limited to the British Isles, but which were evident across Europe? Mistrust may have stemmed from the fact that in a relatively monocultural Europe these exotic itinerants with Indian heritage were perceived as outsiders at odds with convention. Perhaps the persecution was attributable to a desire by the state and capitalist interests to sedentarize labour and reduce the economic power of itinerants (Acton, 1994). Whatever the reasons, legislation sought to restrict or even eradicate nomadic lifestyles, which some critics argue remains a feature of the policy landscape today. A strong collective memory of persecution has shaped community identity and practices for Gypsies and Travellers, and shapes the boundary maintenance between them and the Gorgio (non-Gypsies).

Economic organization based on self-employment and nomadism has been a major factor in maintaining group identity, giving Gypsies and Travellers autonomy and an ability to distance themselves from, and regulate interactions with, those outside the group. The post-war decline in demand for temporary agricultural labour, coupled with the shortage of sites and restrictions on nomadism, mean that itinerant lifestyles are now a less marked feature of being a Gypsy and Traveller. Nevertheless, self-employment remains an important feature of Gypsy and Traveller identity.

Self-employment centred on families helps bond extended family groups, which act as informal employment and information exchanges but also provide a means of passing on skills to younger family members, a process that often takes priority over formal schooling. Hence, Gypsy and Traveller life is marked by a complex set of conventions where economic necessity warrants trading with the Gorgio, but where distance must also be maintained. As Barth (1969) observed, ethnic distinctions do not depend on the absence of social interaction or acceptance, but on the contrary cultural differences can persist despite inter-ethnic contact and interdependence. Mistrust, fear and rejection from mainstream society has contributed to the preservation of Gypsy and Traveller cultural identity. This is clearly illustrated by the full or partial rejection of formal schooling by some Gypsies and Travellers (Derrington and Kendall, 2004).

The lack of involvement in formal schooling on the part of some Gypsies and Travellers combined with the participation of young people in unregulated work (as exemplified in the description of work in a scrapyard) raises concerns about the dangers to which young people might be exposed. Arthur Ivatts, a senior adviser and expert on Gypsy and Traveller education, reflects on the consequences that may follow from not accessing formal education:

> At a societal level, however, the vulnerability [of Gypsies and Travellers] will be considerable. They are more likely to be a burden on the state in terms of health care and social security payments. Some may be involved in petty, or more serious,

criminal activity. Drug abuse and car theft are already reported to be on the increase. At another level, children are frequently involved in dangerous occupations, work long hours, drive heavy vehicles well before age, and use potentially harmful tools and materials. Their parents may also be guilty of breaches in child labour, child protection and health and safety legislation.

(Ivatts, 2005: 13)

Of course, this statement needs to be seen in the context of the experience of formal education of a significant number of Gypsies and Travellers, which is characterized by conflict, bullying and oppression, leading to truancy, academic failure and ingrained mistrust of authority (D'Arcy, 2014). This book will consider questions such as: What should be the ideal relationship between Gypsy and Traveller communities and school? Is it possible to achieve a form of inclusive schooling where Gypsies can retain their identity yet acquire new forms of cultural capital? Indeed, as there is growing evidence that an increasing number of Gypsies and Travellers are embracing formal education, what will be the consequences for identity?

## Boundaries and identity

In the past, distancing from Gorgio society was connected to the Gypsy concepts of taboo and purity, which involve elaborate washing rituals and marimé practices in part related to gender. The anthropologist Judith Okely (1983) claims that these rituals, and the belief that the Gorgio are impure because they do not maintain such rituals, serve to foster a desire for separation. Hawes (1997) asserts that there has been a decline in such cultural notions of pollution, but gender remains an important factor shaping cultural boundaries.

The boundary of an ethnic group is always gendered and often organized around specific gender roles relating to sexuality, marriage and the family. These communal boundaries are often defined by the social expectations that the culture has of women, including honour, purity and mothering, and often symbolize the role of women as an ethnic identity 'marker' (Anthias *et al.*, 1992). Within the Gypsy and Traveller economy, roles have tended to be heavily gendered, with females (young and old) carrying out domestic duties and males (young and old) concentrating on economic activities. Some Gypsy and Traveller teenagers are encouraged to leave secondary school early, thus protecting them from perceived corrupting influences. These fears are particularly acute for females, who are often encouraged to leave school and take up traditional domestic roles (Derrington and Kendall, 2004). Critics argue that such conservatism impinges on the freedom of Gypsy and Traveller women, subjecting them to a double form of discrimination: patriarchal control and the discrimination of dominant society (Kendall, 1997). This book explores the effectiveness of boundary maintenance, including traditional views on participation in school but also the changing nature of gender roles in Gypsy and Traveller communities.

Essentialist views contend that an ethnic or cultural group has a rigid set of characteristics that make up identity and are shared by all members (Woodward, 2000). Others see ethnicity as situational, that is manipulable as circumstances demand or allow (Anthias *et al.*, 1992). Hall (1991; 1992), for example, argues, that identity is not fixed but is a fluid and dynamic concept that can change over time, and syncretize and fuse with other cultures, in turn creating new identities. Identity is not only imposed by others, but also chosen by individuals as part of a sense of belonging.

Identity involves self-reflection, self-perception and agency. Simmel (1957) argues that individuals are not passive tools of culture but creative agents trying to work out the meaning of their lives, and that social life is a struggle and process of tension between individuality and group identity. Bourdieu (1990) argues that identity is formed through both socialization and interaction; self-experience and culture fuse and negotiate responses to events. Bourdieu's position involves acknowledging both the structures within which people negotiate their identity and the role of autonomy and agency. The negotiation between biography and culture can be complex: culture can be more constant than personal biography. It could be argued that such responses are more predictable in times of tension, when an individual may seek greater solace and protection in group identity (Woodward, 2002). Thus, an individual's response to events may be shaped by the nature of those events but they may also find comfort and reassurance within a particular identity. Care needs to be taken, however, in assuming that all cultures and identities are fluid and freely chosen. With these thoughts in mind, the book explores the dynamics of response to challenge and crisis, not just for Gypsies and Travellers, but also for what might be described as white majoritarian culture.

## Moral panics, marginalization and resistance

Over the centuries public attention to Gypsies and Travellers has fluctuated cyclically according to broader social crises and a search for scapegoats. The present moral panic is only the latest recycling of deep-rooted stereotypes. This book seeks to understand the present cycle of moral panic and the exercise of hegemony, which normalizes the ideology of power elites and marginalizes those who diverge. According to Gramsci (1971) counter-hegemonic action requires forms of deliberation and education, and the mobilization of organic as opposed to traditional intellectuals – those at the margins need to be empowered and invested with agency. The book explores what strategies are and might be developed by Gypsies and Travellers in response to marginalization.

It is often at the margins that the greatest injustices of the political order are exposed; awareness of injustice is essential in mobilizing opposition and effecting change. Being at the margins of society can provide some advantage for the excluded, as 'spaces of radical openness' can be formed, removed from the gaze of dominant society (hooks, 1991: 203). Thus, excluded communities occupying marginal space can more readily form an ideology of resistance. What role can Gypsy, Roma and Traveller communities play in counter-hegemonic narratives? Close-bonded family networks, distancing and low levels of formal education have meant that Gypsies, Roma and Travellers often have been at the periphery, yet despite these limitations a relatively long tradition of activism exists within the UK. In 1966 the Gypsy Council, a civil society organization, was founded. A key actor in its early development was a young public-school-educated radical, Grattan Puxon. The Gypsy Council threaded together a number of extended family networks and charismatic leaders into a single campaign, the focus of which was access to decent sites and protection for nomadic lifestyles, as well as access to education – which did not necessarily mean formal schooling. Some campaigners reflected the fears of the families they represented and, although wishing to see greater support for on-site education to nurture literacy and numeracy, they were reticent to sanction initiatives that might lead to greater mainstream educational participation, fearing assimilation and school bullying (Acton *et al.*, 2014). In contrast, other campaigners felt greater access to, and greater participation in, school would give Gypsy and Traveller children the requisite cultural capital to better withstand persecution and assimiliation, and to adapt and innovate (Ivatts with Day, 2014). These tensions were to play a major part in a series of disputes centred on the role of education but also the role of outsiders in the campaign. These disputes bedevilled the Gypsy Council from the 1970s and led to a series of splits in the group (Acton *et al.*, 2014). The issues and fissures raised during this critical period of ethnogenesis remain relevant today and are important themes in this book.

The book responds to questions about activism: Is the Gypsy, Roma and Traveller social movement inclusive enough for the challenges of the twenty-first century? Can activism help protect and maintain Gypsy and Traveller lifestyles? What is the role of outsiders in activist campaigns? Do outsiders speak too much for Gypsy and Traveller communities and inadvertently disempower Gypsies and Travellers themselves? How can those at the margins assume agency and control, and what might be the role of education in emancipatory processes? Conceptions of formal education and cultural capital are important to such discussions, as is Freire's (1971) concept of 'critical pedagogy' or 'conscientization', where connections are made between life experience and the structural nature of inequality, and just as importantly desired change is generated and acted towards. Thus, as Ledwith and Springett (2010) suggest, through critical dialogue and reflection on action, marginalized and oppressed people can move on from a passive, naive 'magical consciousness', which naturalizes the disadvantages in someone's lifeworld (in other words, assumes that injustice is a natural part of the social landscape), to one that envisages transformative change.

## Social policy

To provide context for the narrative of the book, the following section gives an overview of the socio-economic and cultural world views of policymakers. These are centred on moral underclass, social (skills-based) integration and redistributive egalitarian discourses and lead to alternating and fluctuating policies of enforcement, integration and blame.

### *Paternalism and assimilation*

The state has tended to position itself against Gypsy and Traveller communities. Active persecution, as demonstrated in the genocidal policies of the sixteenth and seventeenth centuries, has been punctuated by more subtle forms of coercion resting upon paternalism and notions of 'civilizing', which still represent forms of ethnic cleansing in the sense that they are designed to marginalize and assimilate.

Policies to encourage sedentarization and restrict nomadic lifestyles have been a feature of the policy landscape since the sixteenth century (Kabachnik and Ryder, 2013). Coupled with draconian limitations on nomadism, the formal education of Gypsies and Travellers was viewed by some as a 'civilizing agent', a mechanism to assimilate Gypsies and Travellers. Such views became prominent in the nineteenth century, when the moral zeal of the Christians of the period, combined with the emergence of a strong state apparatus, first seriously brought Gypsies and Travellers to the attention of educators and policymakers.

For some nineteenth-century social reformers, education was a tool by which Gypsies' and Travellers' lifestyles could be reoriented (Mayall, 1988). In this sense education was a more benign part of the continuum of assimilation and violent ethnic cleansing that had existed prior to this time. The church had given its support to the anti-Gypsy laws of the sixteenth century, which sought to outlaw the Gypsy way of life (Acton, 1994). However, from the early nineteenth century there was a change of tack more in tune with the principles of the Enlightenment, which saw the founding of several mission schools for Gypsies and Travellers (Mayall, 1988). For example, the Quakers were interested in settling Gypsies and Travellers in houses as a means of converting them to Christianity and educating their children (Adams *et al.*, 1975).

The most militant advocate for education to facilitate the assimilation and moral reform of Gypsies and Travellers was the social reformer, George Smith of Coalville. In 1883 and 1887 he tried to persuade Parliament to introduce bills to bring education to Gypsy children by requiring Gypsies to register mobile dwellings, which would have enabled school inspectors to bring their powers to bear regarding school attendance (Acton, 1974). This statement reveals Smith's motivation:

> The two main influences I want to bring upon the little travellers and their homes are the universally acknowledged social laws for educating those living in the gutter, viz. ... education and sanitation. ... I want the road to school made easier than the road to jail.
>
> (Cited in Adams *et al.*, 1975: 8)

Smith's proposals were out of step with the laissez-faire political philosophy of the time, and his bills were blocked in Parliament. The Elementary Education Acts issued from 1870, including the Education Act of 1902 that extended compulsory schooling to the whole population, were ineffective in extending education to Gypsies and Travellers (Mayall, 1988). The Children's Act of 1908 required the children of nomadic parents to attend school but for only 200 half-days instead of the normal 400 (Okely, 1983). The official reason was that the state did not wish to interfere with the economic necessity of continued travelling for some Gypsy families. This exception may have been more attributable to a reluctance to see the admission of large numbers of Gypsy students into schools. One of the reasons for the failure of Smith's bills to attract sufficient parliamentary support had been the animosity to such a development, not only from sections of the Gypsy and Traveller community but also from a range of parliamentarians concerned about the impact on their constituents (Mayall, 1988). In fact, the exemption in the 1908 Act was also due to the intervention of Dora Yates, a prominent member of the Gipsy Lore Society, an ethnographic study group. Yates used well-placed political connections to intercede in order to minimize what she believed would be a disturbance to travelling traditions (Okely, 1983). In any case, the authorities rarely enforced the stipulation for partial attendance and few Gypsy children attended school (Kenrick and Bakewell, 1995).

### Statism, the Washington Consensus and the third way

In the post-war period there was growing support for the state to play a central role in economic reconstruction and coordination, and also in welfare provision, which some have termed statism (Ryder, 2015a). The post-war period was shaped by what Levitas (1998) calls the redistributive egalitarian discourse, which underpinned the welfare state and held that poverty was a result of the failure of the economy and that government intervention and redistribution could remedy social ills such as poverty and exclusion.

However, with the ascendancy of the Washington Consensus in the late 1970s, which championed laissez-faire forms of capitalism, statism and most notably intervention and redistribution were derided. A moral underclass discourse (Levitas, 1998) gained traction, a perspective that puts the blame for inequality on the poor themselves. Adherents of this view argue that individual characteristics rather than structural factors are responsible for poverty, implying a pathological model of the poor. Part of the solution to poverty is seen to lie in reducing the role of the state – in particular the range and level of welfare support available to the poor – breaking the culture of poverty where regressive and low aspirational attitudes are transmitted within families. Education has often been viewed as an important tool in countering what are perceived to be the dysfunctional cultural traits of the marginalized.

Such has been the weakness of the left of the political spectrum that faced by the ascendancy of neo-liberalism, it has sought a third way, a non-doctrinaire and technocratic approach that places an emphasis on a social integration discourse (Levitas, 1998), that is the importance of the labour market and specifically of paid work, as the means of inclusion. Critics argue that the focus of this discourse is on the individual and that it represents a 'deficit model', as opposed to focusing on the reform of the structure and nature of society.

These differing interpretations of social exclusion have been prominent in post-war social policy debates but moral underclass and social integration discourses have often been highly influential in responses to Gypsies and Travellers from the state and the wider community. A theme throughout the history of Gypsies and Travellers has been the depiction of this group as criminally and socially deviant. Hence, deficit models that pathologize Gypsies and Travellers have been at the forefront of the state's response to the social exclusion of this group, both in the UK and in continental Europe. Across Europe, policymakers influenced by the culture of poverty theory have advocated compensatory education and training to break the perceived culture of deprivation among Gypsies, Roma and Travellers.

A process of rapid urbanization and development, and greater regulation of open space, took place in the UK in the post-war period. Consequently, Gypsies' and Travellers' traditional stopping places became scarce or access to them was denied (Richardson and Ryder, 2012). At the same time, change was afoot in the rural economy, where the increasing mechanization of agriculture eroded the symbiotic relationship between Gypsies and Travellers and the farming community, where Gypsies and Travellers had secured seasonal labour and stopping places. The economic change and the shortage of stopping places led to an increase in what government called 'unauthorized encampments' – temporary Traveller encampments on disused land (Kabachnik and Ryder, 2013). In some cases, and much to the chagrin of the settled community, such encampments appeared within what they deemed to be their living space: on roadsides, municipal parks and housing estates. Increasingly, these perceived encroachments ignited conflict. In response, in 1968 Harold Wilson's Labour Government supported a private member's bill, tabled by the Liberal MP Eric Lubbock (later Lord Avebury), to establish a duty on local authorities to develop Traveller sites, which were largely council-owned and managed. This became the 1968 Caravan Sites Act.

Despite the fact that successive secretaries of state failed to utilize the available powers to intervene where local authorities failed to provide sites, by the time of the abolition of this duty in 1994, 324 sites had been created, a network of sites that continues to function. Although providing many Gypsy and Traveller families with homes, the statutory duty to provide sites reflected some of the worst aspects of statism by giving tenants little say in the management regimes on such sites, which to the anger of some tenants have been heavily regulated and regimented. In some cases, regulations have undermined the Traveller economy by banning or restraining economic practices, and exorbitant site rents have also undermined the viability of traditional economic practices for some (Ryder and Greenfields, 2010).

Despite the relatively large number of sites developed, the number did not match the demand. Many Gypsies and Travellers, either voluntarily or through compulsion, moved into housing that was largely council controlled, sometimes experiencing profound cultural dislocation and trauma from being placed in a seemingly strange and hostile new world that undermined traditional social networks and coping mechanisms (Cullen *et al.*, 2008). Today, an estimated two-thirds of the Gypsy and Traveller population in the UK occupy housing (Acton *et al.*, 2016).

In the 1990s, a number of Conservative MPs agitated for the privatization of future Gypsy and Traveller site provision (Kenrick and Bakewell, 1995). As a result, the 1994 Criminal Justice and Public Order Act repealed the duty to provide sites. Gypsies and Travellers and campaigning bodies opposed the abolition of the duty. However, the government did introduce Planning Circular 1/94 on Gypsy and Traveller sites. This circular requested that local authorities assist Gypsies and Travellers to identify land they could purchase and develop as private sites. A government circular is less binding than a statutory duty and many councils gave little support to this policy initiative (Richardson and Ryder, 2012).

Given that local authority provision was no longer expanding, Gypsies and Travellers found themselves under pressure due to the lack of vacant local authority pitches. Roadside encampments were not a viable option either, given the ever-present threat of eviction. Increasingly, Gypsies and Travellers mounted retrospective planning applications, where they would purchase land, move on to it and then submit an application (Richardson and Ryder, 2012). The official term for these was 'unauthorized developments'. The growing shortage of pitches on local authority sites led to an increase in unauthorized encampments, escalating conflict and the increasing portrayal of Gypsies and Travellers as 'law breakers' and 'antisocial', particularly by the tabloid press. This reached a peak in the 2005 general election campaign with an intense tabloid campaign against Gypsies and Travellers and the Conservative leader Michael Howard's seven-point charter that advocated greater enforcement against unauthorized encampments and developments (Ryder *et al.*, 2014).

For much of the period of the New Labour Government a steering centralism was evident, that is autonomy within clear parameters, which included targets, directions or state intervention where there was a policy failure at the local level (Ryder, 2015a). This was articulated, for example, in the Labour Government's regional spatial strategies (RSS). In the RSS, great emphasis was placed on local consultation and deliberation feeding into regional accommodation targets, targets that were adjusted at the regional level to reflect broader regional needs and priorities.

With reference to education, post-war economic development and growing urbanization of both authorized and unauthorized sites, as well as the growing movement into housing, led to more Gypsies and Travellers relocating to urban centres. In theory, it was now easier for the children of families living a more sedentary lifestyle to attend school; in spite of this, many still did not. Initially the authorities at both local and national levels made little effort to create equal access for this group or to counter the racism and hostility that Gypsy and Traveller students met in mainstream schools – as is attested by recollections of abuse from those who did attend (Acton *et al.*, 2014).

In the post-war period, calls from policymakers for the educational inclusion of Gypsies and Travellers began to grow. In 1965, the Minister of Housing, Richard Crossman, commissioned a survey of the Gypsy and Traveller population, which found that many were highly nomadic because of the lack of official sites and that as a result few received any form of education (Kenrick and Bakewell, 1995). The educational situation of Gypsy and Traveller children was investigated more thoroughly in the 1967 Plowden Report, *Children and their Primary Schools*. The chair of the investigation, Lady Plowden, stated:

> They [Gypsy and Traveller students] are probably the most severely deprived children in the country. Most of them do not even go to school, and the potential abilities of those who do are stunted ... Improved education alone cannot solve the problems of those children. Simultaneous action is needed by the authorities responsible for employment, industrial training, housing and planning.
>
> (Plowden, 1967: 59)

Commenting on this, Okely (1983) argues that education was closely linked to a programme of integration into industrial waged labour and sedentarization, and that the 1968 Caravan Sites Act rested on statist and assimilationist assumptions that Gypsies and Travellers wanted conventional employment and education. As noted above, these sites were not always popular, as they were located in marginal spaces and governed by a plethora of rules and regulations. In contrast, some observers have asserted that these sites did increase school attendance, as some Gypsies and Travellers saw living on such sites as a contract with the wider community that involved sending their children to school (Adams *et al.*, 1975). An increase in sedentarization among Gypsies and Travellers meant that it was harder for the state to ignore the anomaly of large numbers of Gypsy and Traveller children not attending mainstream education, despite laws that stated that such education should be universal and compulsory (Kenrick and Bakewell, 1995). Access to schools was also increased following the case of Croydon Council, which in 1977 denied access to school to a Traveller child from an unauthorized site. The resulting protest led to the issuing of Government Circular 1/81 calling for local authorities to provide education for all children (Acton *et al.*, 2014). The circular declared: 'The duty embraces in particular travelling children including Gypsies' (Department of Education Circular, 1981: 1/81).

From the late 1960s, Britain began to acknowledge its status as a multicultural society. This recognition of diversity was reflected in various educational reports such as the Swann Report, which not only highlighted the problems of Britain's newly arrived ethnic minorities from its former empire, but also drew attention to the plight of Gypsies and Travellers (Swann, 1985). Thus, policymakers resolved that Gypsies and Travellers, alongside other ethnic groups, were to benefit from a new, multicultural education system that would offer integration and an end to discrimination. One of the most significant developments resulting from this mood was the creation and expansion of Traveller Education Services (TES) in most local authorities (D'Arcy, 2014). They provide support and assistance for schools and Gypsy and Traveller students, and assist in home–school liaison, usually through specialist staff.

### Localism and austerity

Labour's Traveller site delivery policy, based on target setting within regional spatial strategies, prompted sharp criticism, including from the Conservative spokesperson Eric Pickles MP, who subsequently became Secretary of State for Communities and Local Government in the Coalition Government (2010–15). Reflecting the 'new localism', Pickles denounced the RSS as top-down and centralizing government (DCLG, 2010). In recent years, the revival of the concepts of local democracy and participation and the rejection of overt state intervention has become more pronounced and called the 'new localism' (Sullivan, 2012). The Conservatives embraced localism with vigour and allied it to their 'big society' agenda of community action and decentralization. Critics argue that localism has been a convenient slogan to disguise the reality of cutbacks and the culture of small government, reflecting neo-liberal ideals (Kisby, 2010). Austerity and cutbacks in services have been at the heart of central government policy since 2010.

In July 2010, Eric Pickles, then Secretary of State at the Department for Communities revoked Regional Strategies, ostensibly in order to put greater power in the hands of local people rather than regional bodies (Ryder, 2015a). Traveller sites, as well as housing, had formed part of the Regional Strategy targets; now a new localist planning system would come into place, having a major impact on Gypsy and Traveller site provision. One Gypsy described localism as: 'a licence to practise nimbyism; localism allows people to say we're not having Gypsies in our back yard, that's had a detrimental effect in the past' (Ryder and Cemlyn, 2014: 73). There has been an increasing focus on enforcement measures against unauthorized developments and encampments, and for a period all Gypsy and Traveller planning appeals on green belt land were being recovered (reviewed) by the Secretary of State, Eric Pickles. Almost invariably any positive recommendations from planning inspectors were overturned, an act that was eventually ruled as discriminatory in the High Court (Ryder, 2015b). Gypsies and Travellers have felt equally threatened by the Conservative Government's change to Gypsy status in planning law, which stipulates that Gypsies and Travellers must maintain travelling traditions in order to secure planning permission for Traveller sites, a requirement that has alarmed settled families and those too old or sick to travel. It appears that some local authorities are using the new definition to reduce the number of Traveller sites they need to identify and agree to (Hemery, 2016).

Major cuts in local authority expenditure as a result of austerity have led to the fragmentation of local Traveller Education Services, resulting in redundancies and the closure of, or severe reductions in, services. The National Association of Teachers of Travellers has noted:

> The severe cuts to local authorities and the subsequent impact/ demise this has had on a large number of Traveller Education services has made it very difficult to continue this vital work.
>
> (Ryder and Cemlyn, 2014: 137)

## Life strategies

This book provides insights into the impact these policies have had on Gypsy and Traveller lives and the strategies devised to circumvent the policies when they are oppressive. In addition, the book provides a detailed appraisal of more recent policy and explores new directions for inclusive forms of social policy that depart from paternalism and assimilatory agendas. Within this context, education and emancipatory education are important subjects for discussion.

The dramatic economic and social changes of the post-war period have produced a range of responses from Gypsies and Travellers. Acton (1974: 35) devised a typology for the strategies adopted in response to these changes, including: 'conservativism', where Gypsies restrict their interaction with outsiders and cling tenaciously to tradition; 'cultural adaptation', where Gypsies acculturate and are willing to borrow from other cultures; 'passing', where they conceal their Gypsy origins and integrate, and run the risk of assimilation; and 'cultural disintegration', where the experience of acute poverty leads to disorientation and a loss of self-respect and the ability to maintain viable economic practices within the Traveller economy.

These strategies can have consequences for educational participation and are of great relevance to Chapters 3 to 6, which provide descriptions of the lives of Gypsies and Travellers. 'Conservatives' reject formal schooling, particularly in the early or later stages, and continue to prize traditional in-family training and socialization practices. Some Gypsies and Travellers use education as a means to seek out new economic activities and status, yet continue strongly to self-ascribe as Gypsies and Travellers, and retain some or many of the group's traditions and thus acculturate. Those who engage in greater participation in the education system and the other institutions of society may incur the opprobrium of their more traditional peers, who may castigate their adaptation (Derrington and Kendall, 2004).

With particular reference to education and activism, the book uses Acton's typology to explore the causes, trajectories, outcomes and performances of these diverging life strategies in arenas of conflict, for example in schools where relations between the school management and Gypsies and Travellers were strained. It also explores the significance of these strategies for those residing on unauthorized encampments and developments who are on the front line between Gypsies and Travellers and the establishment. Exploration of these trajectories and performances helps to determine the effectiveness of these strategies but also provides some understanding of the outcome they seek. I wish to determine whether 'hope', in a Freirian sense, exists within these strategies. Is a pedagogy of hope evident that transcends critique and cynicism and empowers the prospect of social justice? As Freire noted: 'There is no change without a dream, as there is no dream without hope' (1994: 91). This search and question are central to this book.

# Chapter 3

# Cultural trauma, marginalization and resistance

In the next three chapters I chart life on an urban Traveller site called South Forest and consider its relations with school and the wider community. This chapter provides an overview of life on the South Forest Traveller Site and explores some of the historic and social factors that accentuated the residents' sense of isolation and marginalization. I have used pseudonyms to protect the identities of the people I talk about.

These chapters are highly descriptive of the research field; this detail in my research data enabled me to devise typologies, and the inclusion of some of this material will enable the reader to understand the research field and also make judgements about the soundness of my analysis. The anthropologist Malinowski set a validity rule that readers should have access to a range of materials, including descriptive accounts and statements, so that they can make a fair assessment of the validity of interpretations (cited in Alasuutari, 1998: 63). I have sought to provide this through a 'call to context'; detailing the lived experience of minoritized people.

I gained insight into the South Forest community from the doctoral research described in Chapter 1, which involved working in the local school and organizing youth activities outside of school, some of which took place on the Traveller site. In 'Deep play: Notes on the Balinese cockfight' (1973), Geertz recounts the challenges of being a researcher entering a new world, and describes how, when he and his wife arrived in the Balinese village where they were to undertake anthropological observation, they were treated with caution by the locals, who were wary of the foreign visitors. However, the dynamics of the relationship changed when the couple watched a cockfight together with the villagers in the village square. These competitive jousts are an important element of Balinese culture, and can be viewed as a 'focused gathering' where the participants are engaged in a common flow and are able to relate intensely to each other for a time. However, cockfighting was illegal and the couple's actions during a police raid helped nurture the villagers' acceptance of them. Rather than wave their permits and identification papers at the police, the couple chose instead to flee with the villagers and helped to corroborate alibis when quizzed by the police. This acceptance helped Geertz gain access and insights into Balinese life. As Geertz notes, 'societies like lives contain their own interpretation. One only has to gain access to them' (1973: 86).

Like Geertz, I was initially full of apprehension about whether I would be accepted and was, like Geertz and his wife, met with a degree of wariness and apprehension. I believe that I did gain access and acceptance, and I ascribe this to the effectiveness of some of the youth activities I organized on the site and my willingness to sit and talk for long periods with some of the older residents. These residents were intrigued by my work with other Gypsy communities in the UK and abroad, and may have identified me as something of an outsider, similar to them. These interactions also changed me, and I felt a growing empathy with the plight of this community, which ultimately led me into campaign work for Gypsies and Travellers at a national level (see Chapter 6). In this sense, my interactions with the community elders on South Forest Site, and their acceptance of me, were a subtle means for me to probe my intentions and shape my agenda. In the following three chapters the reader will need to decide whether I retained sufficient critical capacity in my investigation.

There has been a Gypsy community in the vicinity of what is now the South Forest housing estate for centuries. For much of their history in this area, Gypsies lived in the open countryside and practised a traditional nomadic lifestyle, travelling to seasonal employment and fairs. Following the development of a large housing estate at South Forest in the 1960s, Gypsies were forced to seek refuge on the land that the South Forest Site subsequently occupied. The rapid expansion and urbanization programmes of the estate meant that by the late 1960s the Gypsies at South Forest found themselves surrounded by a wall of grey concrete housing estates, and sandwiched between a cement works, a busy road and a canal. In the 1980s the council decided to use the land to create a local authority Traveller site, using government money available for such development. By the time of my observation in 2002, the residents were living on a highly regulated site in close proximity to large numbers of the Gorgio community. This change marked a radical contrast to the way of life the older residents could remember before the urban development of the 1960s, and many of them were angry and resentful about the changes they felt had been imposed upon them. In recent years, conditions on the estate had deteriorated. A report by the Office for Standards in Education (Ofsted), written in 2001, noted that objective indicators identified the area as having high levels of social deprivation.

Gypsies and Travellers living on their own land on private family sites tend to look down on those who live on local authority sites. This statement reveals the sense of superiority felt by some, but also the potential hardships endured on such sites, and the frustrations that were evident at South Forest:

> The Gypsies on these council sites are not part of the settled community and they're not Gypsies either, being stuck on a council site, with all that concrete around them, they're trapped in an enclosure like a dog's kennel, fencing, steel wire, concrete posts, one toilet and shower per family, mother and father having no space for themselves … if you live on a council site like that your hope has gone and you have no hope for your children as your family is going to rot. Wouldn't that depress you? People get in a trap and it's difficult to get out.

Bourdieu (1991a) identified four categories of 'capital' (resources and power): economic capital, social capital, cultural capital and symbolic capital. To this can be added a fifth category, emotional capital (Nowotny, 1981). These classifications will help to provide insights into the nature and extent of the Gypsies' social exclusion and the impact this had on school participation by residents of the South Forest Site.

## Economic capital on the South Forest Site

The Gypsies who lived on the Traveller site were involved in a range of traditional Gypsy trades such as landscape gardening, vehicle repair and construction, but in many cases they worked on a casual basis and alternated between the three activities, being self-employed or working for other Gypsies. The extensive social networks they enjoyed with other Gypsies on the site and within the region often acted as informal labour and commodity exchanges and were an important component of the Traveller economy, whereby work could be found, deals struck and components and machinery sourced. Such social networks have economic value, reducing transaction costs and time and increasing profitability (Ryder and Greenfields, 2010). Many felt contempt for the waged economy. One adult on the South Forest Site said:

> I know a man, he's 'skint' all the time, he works in a factory and lives on the estate, after paying his bills he's got nothing.

He works all hours but what's the point if you've got nothing to show for it. You're better off on the dole.

However, the Traveller economy was fragmenting due to external pressures such as high rents and site restrictions that barred economic activities taking place on pitches as had occurred in the past. Alternative work spaces were difficult and expensive to find. These factors, combined with greater restrictions and regularization of economic activities in terms of registration, reduced the profitability and feasibility of traditional Traveller economic practices. In addition, a lack of formal education greatly reduced their room for manoeuvre and a growing number were dependent on benefits. In the past, divorce and separation had been rare in the Gypsy community but among the Gypsies at South Forest there was a growing number of one-parent (female-headed) families. Just over one-third of the Gypsy students registered at South Forest School had only one parent at home. This was having a negative impact on traditional family socialization practices. Where the father was no longer at home it was harder for the boys to go and work with their fathers. Also, some parents were increasingly nervous about restrictions on child labour and were hesitant to take their boys to work with them until they could pass in appearance for a 16-year old. Instead of working, some of the school non-attenders appeared to be idle, suffering from lethargy and depression. They were in a dangerous vacuum, benefiting neither from formal education nor the socialization practices of their family, leaving them unskilled but also susceptible to low self-esteem and self-confidence and the corresponding dangers that can accompany long-term unemployment: welfare dependency, addiction and even criminality. A number of families were dependent on welfare, some due to health issues. The economic state of the Gypsies in the research field can be classified as decline and stagnation, and this typified the experiences of other Gypsy and Traveller sites and communities (Richardson and Ryder, 2012).

## Social capital and identity on the South Forest Site

Halpern elaborates on the components that make up social capital:

> Most forms, be they kinship, work-based or interest-based, can be seen to have three components. They consist of a network; a cluster of norms, values and expectancies that are shared by group members; and sanctions – punishments and rewards – that help to maintain norms and networks.
>
> (Halpern, 2007: 10)

This section describes the nature of social capital for the Gypsies and Travellers studied but also the sanctions and rewards that helped bind them together, exploring the impact of these variables upon educational participation and identity. Putnam (2000) has broken the concept of social capital into two subtypes: 'bonding' and 'bridging' social capital. Bonding social capital is inward-looking and reinforces exclusive identities and homogeneous groups. Other networks are outward-looking and incorporate people from diverse backgrounds, and can therefore be described as bridging. Both terms are useful in understanding the nature of social capital on the South Forest Site.

Among the Gypsies on the site, social networks were highly bonding. Fellow residents were referred to as cousins and aunts and uncles even where there was not even a tenuous family connection; the residents acted and behaved as if they were one large extended family. As is typical of Gypsies, the maintenance of strong social networks within the site and beyond were cemented by frequent social events such as weddings, baptisms and funerals. The high attendance at these events was attributable to the fact that some of those attending would only have a distant connection with those being christened, married or buried. Traditional conceptions of Gypsy identity involved attendance at fairs, and Gypsies on the site still went to fairs. Some fairs were under threat of closure by hostile local councils. The most important local annual fair for the South Forest Gypsies was held on a nearby village common, near the suburbs of the city but this fair had been banned by the village parish council because of concerns about alleged antisocial behaviour. One pensioner on the South Forest Site exclaimed indignantly with reference to the fair:

> How many get robbed at the Notting Hill festival? How many get knifed? Would they consider closing that festival? No way! But they can go ahead and ban ours!

Some of the older Gypsies still spoke the Romany language but it was in decline among the young. As is typical of Gypsy culture, some still had an avid interest in horses and even kept horses in nearby fields, but this was a practice under pressure. Site rules meant that horses could no longer be kept on the pitches and development proposals threatened the possibility of keeping horses in the nearby fields. As has been said, for a growing number of families the Traveller economy was under severe pressure. Furthermore, although occupying caravans, many on the site were now largely static as the options and feasibility of nomadism were greatly impeded by a lack of stopping places and government restrictions on unauthorized encampments.

Some of the Gypsies, in particular the older ones, felt that things were changing on the South Forest Site and that the younger generations were losing their Gypsy identity. One day, three Gypsy pensioners reminisced about life in the open countryside, where many families had lived prior to moving to South Forest, and how they had had unlimited freedom to travel and live unfettered by bureaucracy. One sighed and exclaimed: 'They have listed buildings but soon they will need to have us listed. We're a dying breed.' The differences between the young and the old were dramatic. Some of the older Gypsies clung to conservative moral values, but young girls on the site were no longer covering their legs in long skirts as Gypsy women had been expected to in the past but were wearing short miniskirts and tight, low-cut tops like their peers on the estate. This was a visible indicator of the growing influence of the outside world but also evidence of the growing freedom of some women within the Gypsy community. In part, the site itself and the way residents were made to live were blamed for what some considered to be negative change. Some of the older Gypsies despaired about the South Forest Site. They referred to it as a 'reservation' and complained that it was something that held them in stasis, and spelt the end of many traditional lifestyle practices. One female pensioner bemoaned the changes:

> These young ones on the site, they're not real Gypsies any more; they don't know any of the old ways. The girls, for example, they wouldn't know how to knock on doors and make a living. The truth is they're all Gorgio: they mix with kids on the estate and even marry them.

Cultural customs and practices, although important, were not the central features of group identity nor the force that maintained it, and adaptations by the young were not a real threat to group cohesion. A fear of the wider community and an elaborate series of rewards and sanctions were the foundations upon which strong-bonded identity was built. Identity is increasingly fragmented and fractured (Hall and Du Gay, 1997). No cultural or ethnic group is static: each generation is subjected to new experiences and even environments that the previous generation did not experience, leaving in their train an imprint reflected in new tastes, views, aspirations and even outward appearance. Barth noted how individuals could participate in different 'streams of tradition' or 'universes of discourse', with varying depth and intensity (Jenkins, 1996). Dramatic changes had taken place for many Gypsies and Travellers across the country. In the case of the South Forest Gypsies, within 50 years they had moved from a state where they lived a truly nomadic lifestyle to one where they occupied houses on a large modern housing estate or pitches on the highly regulated local authority site. These major changes were bound to have an impact on traditional lifestyles and create new environmental and cultural influences. However, a sense of difference is at the core of many people's cultural identity and this perception is at its clearest when standing at the boundary of that culture. As Jenkins (1996) has noted, this leads to an awareness that things are done differently 'there' (across the boundary) and the sense of threat that poses for how things are done 'here' (within the group). The Gypsies on the South Forest Site had sought to diminish the influences of these external factors by maintaining as far as possible a cultural distance between their lives and those of the wider community.

Distance was maintained through a sense of fear and mistrust of the wider community. Derrington and Kendall (2004) note that this contempt can be equal in its intensity to that held by house-dwellers for Gypsies. Putnam (2000) argues that positive and negative interventions in the lives of groups and individuals can have a corresponding effect on trust formation, civic engagement and reciprocity in the wider community. Given the culturally traumatic experiences of South Forest Gypsies it was not surprising that their trust in the wider community was low and that they looked to themselves and their own kind for strength and security. Suspicion of outsiders and the wider estate had increased in recent years and were reflected in the fear that the Gypsies had of the world beyond the site. One of the Gypsy boys had recently been knifed and one group were said to have been shot at by a Vietnamese 'gangster', an act that intensified the Gypsies' fear of the estate. A Gypsy father who lived on the site expressed this fear and suspicion:

> When my boy got stabbed, that was attempted murder. All along this road were crime notices asking people if they saw any crime, but did they come forward for my boy? No, of course not! They didn't because he's a Gypsy. They hate Gypsies, that's what it comes down to. You can be a Hindu or asylum seeker and they will happily live next door to them and they won't give them any grief. They love that, but if you're a Gypsy they'll slam the door in your face.

Most people on the estate kept their distance from the site; they perceived it as a dangerous and unwelcome place. A pensioner site resident noted the fears of the wider community and used an argument common among Gypsies and Travellers that explained the fear but also the low opinion of the Gorgio community held by many on the site:

You won't get more villains than what are on that estate. When a Traveller has a 'punch-up' that's it – it's all over and they are friends again, but I see in *The Sun* that there was a shoot-out on the M4. I bet they weren't Travellers. These football matches, who does the shooting and stabbing there? Who killed Blakelock on Broadwater Farm? Was it a Traveller? How many times do you read in the paper, Gypsy people leaving their children? Or treat them bad and neglect them? We are a race of people that think the world of our children!

Many of the Gypsies were especially concerned by the racial diversity of their neighbourhood, which had in recent years become more diverse through migrations of refugee groups including Vietnamese, Kosovans and Somalis. Ryan *et al.* (2008) have noted the power of 'constrict theory', which argues that increased diversity appears to reduce levels of trust and wider community participation. According to Putnam (2000), diversity can lead people to withdraw from collective life. Thus a number of fears combined with mistrust led to low levels of bridging social capital with the wider community, which was translated into civic disengagement but that was balanced with close social bonding among their co-ethnics.

One Gypsy parent stated, 'I'm all for our kids mixing with non-Travellers, but those kids from the estate are coming on to the site and getting them into bad ways.' The reality was, though, that whether or not these children were getting into 'bad ways', their interaction in school and in the wider community with non-Travellers was minimal. Not only did they keep their distance but they shared the fears and suspicions of their elders towards outsiders, despite their superficial interaction with wider mainstream culture through fashion and music. This was reflected, for example, in the reluctance of many students on the South Forest Traveller Site to participate in secondary school or to socialize with other groups, within and outside school. An employee with the Traveller Education Service noted the impact of bonding social networks on school participation: 'The greatest problem for boys on the site is peer pressure: for some, setting off for school in their school uniform with a satchel on their backs sets them up for ridicule from those who are not going to school.' A Gypsy student who had stopped attending school informed me: 'The thing is, we tend to go along with what all the others do. Once one lot stop going to school, all the others stop as well; we stick together and do things together.'

Despite generational differences, the Gypsies on the South Forest Site were a cohesive and bonded group who maintained distance between themselves and outsiders and shared the profound suspicions of their elders for newer arrivals on the estate, such as the Kosovans, Vietnamese and Somalis. Halpern (2007) could be right in claiming that being told not to trust others by your parents and elders can have a profound and lasting effect.

Being part of a strong bonding community could hold a number of incentives. Durkheim (1997) argues that communities typified by strong social bonds enjoy high levels of mutual support, which impacts positively on physical and mental health indicators. Correspondingly, a decrease in bonding social capital could be counterproductive to the happiness and well-being of a Traveller. The Noble family had had to leave the site in the 1990s as the number of pitches were reduced when the council created a local authority site. Like other displaced families, the Nobles moved into social housing on the estate. The Nobles felt strange and isolated in housing. For a number of years Mr Noble slept in a small trailer caravan parked in the car park of the tower block where they lived because he was unable to sleep in the flat. The Nobles were desperate to return to the site. They were on the waiting list and were frequent visitors to friends and family on the site. Their sense of frustration was as profound as that of those who lived on the South Forest Site.

Sanctions can play a powerful role in the maintenance of group norms (Posner and Rasmusen, 1999). The Gypsies on the site were said by Simon James (South Forest Traveller Education Service) to have resented those who had left the site and moved into housing, and believed the housed families had turned their backs on their culture. Thus, a move from the close-knit community on the site could lead to a loss of status (symbolic capital) and sense of being a Gypsy in the eyes of their peers. Though rich in the density of their bonding social capital, the deterioration of economic capital and diminishing cultural and symbolic capital in their eyes and those of the wider community influenced some Gypsies to deviate from prescribed norms and embrace change. Living in housing or working in the waged economy led to the development of new coping strategies, which included greater participation in formal schooling and bridging social capital where networks and ties were developed with people outside their ethnic group. Such ties, though, were not intense, for the estates on which they resided were typical of those located in neighbourhoods with high levels of social exclusion and were characterized by low levels of community engagement and interaction (Byrne, 2005). Where interaction did take place, it often involved those Gypsies living in housing hiding their ethnicity from their neighbours and work colleagues, and thus opened the door to possible erosive doubts and uncertainties about their culture and identity, a psychological consequence of internalizing such negative perceptions.

## Emotional capital on the South Forest Site

Nowotny (1981) drew on Bourdieu's conceptual framework of capital and developed the term 'emotional capital', a variant of 'social capital' that was characteristic of the private sphere as opposed to the public, and confined within the bounds of affective relationships of family and friends providing emotional support. For Nowotny, this capital is heavily gendered: it is a resource women have in greater abundance. On the South Forest Site in particular, where strong bonding relations existed, emotional capital was characterized by strong feelings of concern and protection for their young and concern and empathy at the unfair treatment they felt was meted out by school. These emotional expressions did not, though, seem to be stronger among females; such was the collective nature of the community and the emphasis placed on the welfare of children that these emotions were equally strong among men and women. Reay comments on emotional capital and the impact it can have on interaction with school:

> My research data indicated a very thin dividing line between empathy and over-identification when children were experiencing difficulties in school. Many mothers talked poignantly of their concern at children's distress. However, while it was natural for mothers to share in children's feelings of anxiety and unhappiness, if they became too enmeshed in children's distressed feelings they were often left both unable to provide appropriate support and having to deal with a welter of negative feelings of their own.
>
> (Reay, 2004: 62)

When applied to the relations between Gypsy parents and school, these comments are revealing. A strong sense of emotional capital often led parents to side with and support their children in disputes with school with an intensity that led the school to classify them as anti-school. Parents also condoned non-participation in school, but rather than being viewed as a deficit-model it should perhaps be perceived as a mechanism for avoiding low self-esteem and anxiety (symbolic violence), features which they felt were prevalent in school.

## Cultural capital on the South Forest Site

Cultural capital consists of the competencies, skills and qualifications of a group that can be transmitted to younger group members via institutions such as the family and school (Bourdieu, 1990). As is the case with economic capital, there is not an even distribution of cultural capital. Bourdieu argues that the family socialization process, language and cultural customs of the group can favour some groups over others. For Bourdieu the education system, which prizes academic theory and competition through the exam system, favours the dominant classes in society who are more culturally equipped to succeed within these parameters as they possess the language and cultural insights and outlooks (dispositions) to navigate their way successfully through the formal education system. The academic system appears to foster fairness and meritocracy, but through the exam process the class system reproduces itself and political and economic capital is transferred from one generation to another. Participants in the school system begin with different handicaps based on cultural endowment, so the process fosters and maintains privilege. This leads to low-income and disadvantaged groups often faring poorly in school, where other types of knowledge are not classified as legitimate, accorded status and rewarded (Jenkins, 2007).

Many of the Gypsies on the site prized interactive skills learning. A primary socialization tool was in-family training, and the ideal was for young Gypsies to learn skills by working with their families. A favoured strategy was for boys to help their fathers or members of their extended family in the family business from a young age, in some cases dropping out of school before the school leaving age to undertake such work, while girls worked within the family unit undertaking childcare and domestic duties. Many of the Gypsies considered this heavily gendered and practical socialization process to be a more effective tool of preparation for adulthood than school. One Gypsy of pensioner age commented:

> If a bloke's son left school at 14, he was in the blacksmith shop with his father and the father would show the boy the trade and in three months he would know the trade like his father, but now boys have to go to college to learn the trade. Whatever can a boy learn about shoeing by looking at a piece of paper? Daft!

Many on the site, both men and women, shared such sentiments; one mother declared:

> All they are interested in, like with my boy John, is just being a tree surgeon. Now and then he will go with his father for the day; he won't get no better experience than that rather than sitting

around at that school. When he gets into that lorry he learns what a man should do.

As well as rejecting the value of formal education, many of the Gypsies and Travellers in the research field were unable to foster the cultural dispositions and academic foundations that would enable their children to achieve academic success. Many of the parents had low levels of education and disrupted educational histories, and some were illiterate. Levels of parental education are major determiners for a child's educational attainment. The local secondary school reflected the deprivation of the neighbourhood and had attainment rates below the national average and a high turnover of staff. The school was classified by Ofsted as working in 'challenging circumstances', and had in the past received critical inspection reports. Thus, the economic capital of the Gypsy and Traveller parents impacted on where they lived and therefore the quality of the education that they could access, and participation and attainment in school were low. Also, there was a clear divide between the attitudes and performance in school of Gypsy students from the site and those in housing, with those in housing being more proactive in their support of school (see Chapter 4).

## Symbolic capital on the South Forest Site

Symbolic capital is prestige and honour, and in communities this can be translated into power. In his study of the Kabyle in Algeria, Bourdieu reflects on the significance of a sense of honour:

> struggles for recognition are a fundamental dimension of social life ... what is at stake in them is an accumulation of a particular form of capital, honour in the sense of reputation and prestige, and there is therefore a specific logic behind the accumulation of symbolic capital.
>
> (Bourdieu, 1990: 22)

Symbolic capital was an important feature of the cultural framework of many of the Gypsies on the site. Symbolic capital could be maximized by conforming to the 'Gypsy and Traveller way'. Conformity to this 'habitus', a set of dispositions and classifications, impacted on thoughts and actions, and a successful navigation of these could increase status and reputation but also the maintenance of group goals and identity; those who deviated from these suffered a corresponding loss of status. The importance of symbolic capital created divisions between the Gypsies: those who were housed tended to conform to the norms of school and sought to achieve conventional exam-based success; those who resided on the site tended to resist school through non-attendance or through non-conformity to prescribed norms within school.

According to Bourdieu and Wacquant (2002), when a holder of symbolic capital uses the power against an agent who holds less capital, and seeks to change their actions, they inflict symbolic violence. It can be argued that in the wider field the Gypsies suffered from profound symbolic violence from a hostile society that viewed their life patterns with extreme hostility and suspicion. Furthermore, in the view of a significant number of the Gypsies on the South Forest Site, a range of institutions including schools were seeking to impose alien and unwelcome influences on their collective cultural dispositions and therefore imposing symbolic violence. It was this perception that in part inspired resistance to school and a suspicion of the wider community.

## Cultural trauma

Giddens (1996) terms the present age one of 'reflexive modernity', in which ordinary social actors feel that society has changed rapidly and that the future is uncertain. This is an age unlike 'modernity', which was based on absolute truths and certainties. This mood of anxiety and uncertainty caused by fundamental change was prevalent among the adult Gypsies on the South Forest Site. My survey of the economic, social, cultural and symbolic capital of the Gypsies and Travellers in the research field revealed a high level of dislocation. For them, change had been more profound than it had been for the wider community. In the post-war period the interventions in the lives of Gypsies and Travellers by the state and mainstream society had been significant, leading to a movement from relatively unfettered nomadism to stasis in housing or on local authority sites, and from self-employment to waged labour or welfare dependency. This change can be seen as a form of cultural trauma:

> Cultural trauma occurs when members of a collectivity feel they have been subjected to a horrendous event that leaves indelible marks upon their group consciousness, marking their memories forever and changing their future identity in fundamental and irrevocable ways.
>
> (Alexander *et al.*, 2004)

Cultural trauma is a powerful phenomenon that can be transmitted from one generation to another in terms of its influence on perceptions and interactions with others. Thus slavery, though abolished 150 years ago, continues to exert influence on the psyche of Black Americans to this day (Eyerman, 2004). Such trauma does not always come from sudden change: dramatic change can happen over an extended timescale and sometimes only in the wake of that change does trauma appear. Caruth states that such trauma is:

> a blow to the basic tissues of social life that damages the bonds attaching people together and impairs the prevailing sense of communality. The collective trauma works its way slowly and even insidiously into the awareness of those who suffer from it, so it does not have the quality of suddenness normally associated with 'trauma'. But it is a form of shock all the same, a gradual realisation that the community no longer exists as an effective source of support and that an important part of the self has disappeared.
>
> (Caruth, 1996: 187)

For Gypsies and Travellers, including those discussed in this chapter, the change that had occurred in their lives can be described as 'traumagenic'. According to Sztompka (2004), 'traumagenic change' occurs within a relatively short period of time, is wide and comprehensive, touching many aspects of life, and fundamentally touching core aspects of social life or personal fate. The adult Gypsies in this chapter are 'carriers of cultural legacy' (Sztompka, 2004): these are the generations that were socialized, indoctrinated and habituated in a particular cultural milieu. What was most evident in the life stories of many of the adult Gypsies I spoke to on the South Forest Site was that a sense of stability and order had been taken away from them and that change had been unwelcome and imposed. Tom Burrage, was one such resident. He was in his late 30s, had lived all his life on the site and had a large family with five children. Tom was finding life difficult; his car repair business was not going well and the family were in financial hardship. One day Tom complained:

> I feel like I'm in a rut, I can't move forward but want to, I want to be known by people as Mr Burrage not that Gypsy on the site. I want my children to have a better way of life than me and to have a decent cheque in their pocket at the end of the month.

Tom also felt powerless and under threat on the site because of the weak tenancy rights and the perceived authoritarian management style of the site manager. Tom despaired:

> What a lot of people don't know is that [the site manager]
> terrorizes people, even some of the young children go screaming
> to their mothers when he comes up the road here, … it doesn't
> help, when [the site manager] says 'If you don't clear up your
> pitch in seven days, you'll get evicted'. That's no way to treat
> people! When you go around these council estates you can see
> old cars on the forecourts, caravans and stuff but they don't
> bother about them! Listen, our site manager, he's supposed to be
> a Gypsy liaison officer but I never voted for him for that, no one
> asked me if it was OK for him to be here. When we want to get
> hold of him to tell him something is wrong, he's never here, he
> hasn't got time, but if someone complains about us he's on to it
> fast, like with me when I had a bit of rubbish outside my pitch.

Tom was also extremely scornful about the secondary school and the
security they could provide for his children, and believed that the school
authorities were powerless to deal with the transgressions of students from
other ethnic minorities, or even turned a blind eye to them. However, Tom
felt that they were overzealous to the point of being prejudiced in punishing
Gypsy students. The following comment from Tom was typical in revealing
his low opinion of the school:

> Those asylum seekers from Kosovo, they can do what they want
> in school. One day one of them brought in a six-inch knife and
> the teachers pretended nothing had happened but my boy went
> in with a penknife and was excluded. Those asylum seekers get
> everything and we get nothing.

Gypsies such as Tom were no different from the working-class supporters
of the radical right-wing British National Party on the South Forest Estate
responding to perceived unfair treatment and exclusion. With both groups,
the unsavoury nature of their racism should not deflect from the fact that the
primary cause of the reactionary positions they adopted was the structural
inequalities from which they suffered. Comments such as these led the school
to label Tom a racist. Tom, like many Gypsies on the South Forest Site,
had little regard for the formal curriculum of school. His contempt for the
school was demonstrated in a story that the head teacher recounted to me:

> Tom brought Fred into school one day. They were actually going
> out for the day as a family and had gone to the pie shop and
> something wasn't right and Fred had to share with Nell (his
> sister) and Fred threw a 'wobbler' and Tom said 'right, that's it,

you're going to school', so he brought Fred screaming the place down shouting 'I don't want to stay here'. Tom was shouting, 'That's your punishment, you're not coming home with us because you've been bad'. It's all quite amusing but clearly it says something about the way in which they see school.

Although critical of authority in the guise of the site manager and the school, Tom appeared hesitant and unsure about assuming greater control over his affairs. With several residents I raised the notion of a residents' association on the site but Tom, who could read and write, stated that such an association would only work if there was someone like me to head it. The notion of acting as an advocate for the whole site and directly raising concerns with the authorities was something that residents such as Tom shied away from. One resident of the site explained such inertia:

> They don't have the confidence to do it for themselves, a lot of them can't read or write or they don't know how to speak in a meeting; they need help and support.

Tellingly, the site manager opposed the idea, claiming that a committee had existed in the past when the council first assumed control of the site. It had had the function of offering advice on the site's redevelopment but all people had done was talk over each other and the meetings lacked coherence.

Residents such as Tom had experienced traumagenic change. They were deeply wary of outsiders and authority, and appeared to have little optimism for the future. The old coping strategies, in particular economic ones, were failing and Tom had no clear strategy for him and his family to move forward. The Gypsies who had moved from the site into housing appeared to have largely embraced waged employment and schooling. As noted earlier, there was a perception on the site that those who had moved into housing had somehow let the community down. For some, housing posed a cultural danger. One elderly site resident exclaimed:

> Travellers don't want it [nomadism] to die out, they would love it to come back, everyone you talk to, they'd love to travel but you go into a council house and after two years that's your lot, you're finished. It's like putting a wild bird in a cage. Gypsies were never made for houses, they like to roam free.

Some of those living in housing had lived deeply traditional Gypsy lifestyles in their childhoods. The Manley family were one of the many housed families that I came to know. Nora Manley, the family matriarch, had been raised within a nomadic Gypsy lifestyle but frequent eviction and growing hardship had persuaded her father to move into a council house when she was 12. Her husband had been born in a bender (a traditional Gypsy tent made from branches and canvas) in woodland that was now part of the South Forest housing estate. Now the Manleys lived in a house on the estate and their only child, Eve, attended South Forest School.

Eve was in Year 9 (age 14), had an above average attendance rate and attainment and was an active participant within the school community, for example writing for the school magazine. It was her ambition to become a journalist. The Manleys still considered themselves to be Gypsies. Nora had trained Eve in the use of the Romany language and she was able to hold a conversation in Romany. Eve felt herself to be a Gypsy and believed that this would not change with academic or career success: 'If I become a journalist and even live in a house, I will still be a Gypsy.' For Nora, living in a house did not impact on her ethnicity:

> Many of my family still live in caravans or on sites. I think
> because we are in a house it doesn't make any difference at all but
> I want, how can I put it in the right way? I want the best for Eve.

The last part of this statement indicates a perception that Eve was better placed to access the opportunities of mainstream society by living in a house. The same view is evident in another comment by Nora:

> I do miss travelling. It was a good life. I'm not saying it wasn't but
> we've settled down on the estate now and have a nice house; at
> the end of it all though we want what's best for Eve.

Nora acknowledged that many of their neighbours did not recognize them as Gypsies, no doubt because they did not openly advertise the fact and because they did not conform to traditional stereotypes of Gypsies. When I interviewed Eve, she said she would be reluctant for a teacher to make a reference to her ethnicity in a lesson, a factor that also demonstrates unease about the expression of ethnicity outside the family unit. A comment from Eve about the South Forest Site students who did not attend school also indicated a desire that was common among the housed Gypsies to distance themselves from the site:

> They just don't like coming to school, they like lying in bed,
> they're just lazy. Mum says they're stupid, they won't learn
> anything. Most of them can't even read or write.

Given the greater levels of interaction with wider society that result from acculturation, the number of incidents in which expressions of ethnicity are suppressed may be great, due to the strong anti-Gypsy sentiments evident in wider society. Contact with these sentiments, or the fear of such, and even the internalization of these negative views could have damaging implications for self-ascription, leading to possible assimilation. It could also curtail the effectiveness of acculturation as a process that can preserve at least the outlines of identity by assisting adaptation, which can make such an identity continue to be socially and economically viable.

Part of the continued attraction in ethnicity lies in the fact that in late modernity society has failed to successfully transfer to the state the sense of mutual responsibility and obligation that is evident in kin groups. As such, values in the state are based on an abstract allegiance to a set of principles rather than on a set of people (Guibernau and Rex, 1997). The stubborn, albeit differentiated, retention of identity as espoused by Tom Burrage and Nora Manley suggests that ethnic identity satisfies a deep-seated need and provides a compass and an anchor in an environment of cultural turbulence and dislocation. A strong kinship group and sense of identity provides not only comfort but also a sense of protection against perceived enemies

The actors featured in these profiles did not blindly perform their actions like automata in accordance with a set of mechanistic rules. Their 'habitus', a shared body of dispositions and classifications (Bourdieu, 1995) that had been shaped by their socialization and membership of the Gypsy community, among other influences, impacted on the strategies they chose to adopt. Within this framework, though, there was room for personal agency, and improvisation and adaptation. Furthermore, habitus can produce very different practices depending on what is going on in the changed environments, leading to new strategies and improvisations. Hence Nora was able to depart from perceived collective norms and live in a house and encourage her daughter to accrue academic success. However, I sometimes felt that families such as the Manleys had responded to the growing restrictions and restraints placed on Gypsy lifestyles by believing that moving into a house was a lifeline that could enable them to adopt alternative strategies such as waged labour and mainstream school yet simultaneously retain their Gypsy identity. However, they had been compelled to make radical departures from tradition, which led to the risk of them retaining a superficial and timid form of identity that made them susceptible to assimilation.

Bourdieu (2006) argues that certain perceptions are formed by the working class as a consequence of negative experiences in the economic system, the intensity and frequency of which forge a perception carried into the present from the past. So it was with Tom Burrage that displacement and dislocation nurtured a profound mistrust of majority society that shaped his relations with authority and institutions.

To borrow from Merton's classification of responses to social trauma and social change, there are four typical adaptations: innovation, rebellion, ritualism and retreatism (Merton, 1996). These are redolent of the typology Acton devised for diverging Gypsy and Traveller life strategies of: conservatism, cultural adaptation, passing and cultural disintegration. The traditional Gypsies on the South Forest Site displayed forms of conservativism but in some cases, in particular where the Traveller economy was failing, there was a risk of cultural disintegration. Many of the housed families displayed cultural adaptation but also a danger of passing (assimilating). These diverging strategies and their implications for school participation are the theme of the next chapter.

# Chapter 4

# School: Resistance and conflict

This chapter describes the educational experiences of Gypsies within South Forest School, providing insights into the mismatch between the curriculum and Gypsy identity and aspirations. In turn, the chapter outlines how school misconceptions about Gypsies and Travellers contributed towards exclusion and alienation

## Introduction

As a major agent of socialization, school represents an arena where conflict, when it occurs, may be an indicator of fundamental differences between a minority and a majority culture. This comment from a Gypsy parent provides insights into some of the tensions that existed between residents of the South Forest Traveller Site and South Forest Secondary School:

> What puts a lot of Travellers off [school] is the way they are treated there when they get there. Take Tim boy and Frankie [two of his children]: if they fight with other boys, they don't get sent the notes but they come to us, saying your boys have been fighting. It's all with the Travellers, they're all against the Travellers, it don't matter where you go. It started off years and years ago, when Gypsies used to travel around: they had their stopping places but people would say, 'if you go down the lane tonight there are Gypsies there.' Right back to the Stone Age they have turned against Gypsies, 'lock your children up tonight, Gypsies are down the lane', that's what they done.

For many of the residents on the site the school was a prominent agent of exclusion, and consequently relations between the site and school were extremely strained. One student from the site informed me: 'They [the staff] hate us because we are different from the way they are. I hate nearly every teacher in this school.' Such complaints were common among the parents and children resident on the site.

There were approximately 40 Gypsy students in the school. The numbers were actually higher but low rates of self-ascription hindered the identification of an accurate figure. A group within South Forest School that I termed the 'resisters' (approximately 16), who were largely resident on the South Forest Site, had a low opinion of the curriculum and school staff. The resisters had low levels of achievement and poor attendance; exclusion and expulsion rates were also very high. The 'semi-accommodated' (approximately 7) maintained a more strategic approach and took part in occasional poor behaviour on a minor scale. Such an approach meant they were not labelled as ultra-school conformists by their peers and school, yet on the other hand they were able to generally subscribe to the ethos of the school. The 'mainstreamers' (approximately 14) had a very good level of attendance and a high level of conformity to the ethos of the school. They demonstrated a desire to stay until 16, and the females in particular expressed an intention to study in further or higher education. The 'assimilated' no longer subscribed to Gypsy identity and often held negative views of, or no interest in, Gypsy identity (approximately 3, but numbers were probably much greater). Generally, the mainstreamers, semi-accommodated and assimilated lived in housing but there were exceptions across these classifications.

At South Forest School, few of the housed Gypsies self-ascribed in school ethnic monitoring. They described themselves as White British in ethnic monitoring forms but in conversation with me many would ascribe as Gypsies. The Gypsies at South Forest School were far from being a homogeneous group; as discussed in the Chapter 3, many of the site residents appeared to be at odds with those in housing, who were more willing to conform and participate in school and the wider community. This conflict also extended towards the school. This chapter describes the causes and nature of this conflict.

## Management

Research has shown that senior management in a school play a key role in influencing the extent of educational inclusion by setting the tone or ethos of the school and by strengthening policies to alleviate social and racial exclusion by vigorously supporting them throughout the school (Gillborn, 1990). The following section attempts to provide insights into the management philosophy of South Forest School.

The school operated in what Ofsted describe as 'challenging circumstances', that is, it served a catchment area characterized by high levels of deprivation and disadvantage. This clearly presented the school's management with serious attainment and pastoral challenges. At the same time, the management and staff in the school were under acute pressure to raise academic standards as a consequence of education reforms and were particularly sensitive to their standing in school league tables, especially in terms of GCSE results. Such results influenced the perceptions of the school by the community they served and impacted on enrolment rates and thus the income and the future of the school. Furthermore, the attainment profiles of the school also shaped the key outcomes of the inspection process by Ofsted. South Forest School had once failed an inspection.

The local authority responsible for South Forest School intended to turn the school into an academy. Academy schools are state-funded schools that are run outside of local authority control and that can receive support from private sponsors. South Forest School reacted to the proposal to create an academy by campaigning to persuade the local authority to support its own plans for an academy, which unlike the local authority plan would retain the existing management team. This campaign required a great deal of time and energy from the school management team, in particular on initiatives to raise attainment, such as greater academic streaming. Senior staff felt that an improved attainment profile would be central to maintaining the school, and its leadership, in their present form. A number of teacher informants who were wary of both academy proposals felt the incessant campaigning and attainment-driven focus of the management team was to the detriment of groups such as the Gypsies, as the school was distracted from addressing fundamental problems that existed within the school that in an ideal world could have been addressed through reducing teacher:student ratios and increasing resources.

At times the school management appeared to view the difficult relations with the Gypsy parents and students as a serious nuisance that threatened to undermine attempts to save their vision of the school's future, perceiving the parents and students from the South Forest Traveller Site as being troublesome and antisocial. So fixated was the school on this particular cohort that the management were unaware of the existence of the sizeable and generally conforming 'mainstreamer' group. In the opinion of the management, the required response to the recalcitrance of the Gypsies was the implementation of firm sanctions. The following comment from Steve Cartwright, the head teacher, concerning serious tensions within the school between Gypsy and other students a year earlier, reveals such sentiments:

> I had a largish group of Travellers banding together in school and they were not being 'put upon', they were being bullying, aggressive and violent and other children were just terrified

of them and there were a couple of occasions when they were rampaging all around the building, so I just adopted this position on things, namely, you don't take the law into your own hands here, so I thought if I said it enough the message would get through. I can't help the fact it's against the way someone's culture is, I feel nobody has the right to treat other people like that and I have a responsibility to all children in the school to ensure they are not terrified when they come here.

The statement demonstrates several stereotypical images of Gypsies and Travellers, who are perceived as being 'lawless' and 'intimidating'. Some teacher informants felt that the head teacher had adopted a polarized view of the tensions and was failing to acknowledge the legitimate grievances of the Gypsies. Instead, the head teacher blamed the deterioration in relations and engagement with school on the Gypsies themselves. Thus, the head teacher felt his policy, which resulted in high levels of exclusion from school for this minority, was vindicated. As a result of this stance, the school management team ignored the advice of the Traveller Education Service to repair the fractured relations between the school and the Gypsy community by employing the local authority mediation service, as local authority guidance recommended, or by initiating dialogue. This recalcitrance may have prolonged the dispute, as research has shown that third-party interventions can enable concessions to be made in a dispute without loss of face to the opposing factions, thus promoting more rapid conflict resolution (Hare *et al.*, 1995).

## Classroom management and curriculum

A majority of the lessons observed were teacher-centred, where the focus was on the teacher, with the students expected to play a passive role. The classrooms were usually set out with formal rows of desks, again reflecting traditional teaching concepts. In this formalized classroom environment, the teacher would often set a series of written tasks based on reading and writing skills. Discussion, drama and other more creative activities were kept to a minimum. A long-standing member of staff acknowledged the formalism of much of the teaching that took place within the school:

It's a question of resources. Flexibility in the classroom takes a lot of experience. Teaching now is very demanding because of all the demands, such as discipline, planning and bureaucracy. It's very stressful! No wonder so many teachers don't make it to the end.

Such formal approaches to teaching seemed to be dictated by the demands of the national curriculum, which meant that large amounts of information needed to be transmitted from the teacher to the student. Furthermore, there was a high turnover of staff and many of the teachers were relatively new to the profession. For some of these teachers, lacking experience and confidence, and others burdened by the demands and challenges of national curriculum teaching, such formal teaching provided the best means of covering the curriculum with minimal planning and for the teachers offered the best form of control of large and at times unruly classes.

In discussions, many of the Gypsy students expressed dissatisfaction with the quality of their learning experiences in the classroom. Nearly all the students expressed greater appreciation of their time at primary school where they felt that relationships with teachers had been stronger. In contrast, at secondary school moving from one class to another and having a large number of teachers was unpopular. The sentiments of many of the Gypsy and Traveller students interviewed are expressed in the following comments by one Gypsy student: 'The teachers were better at primary school. They didn't shout at you all the time like they do now.' Frequent discontent was voiced by students about the poor relationship between teachers and students, where threats and shouting to maintain discipline were common. One student exclaimed: 'They're "moany" and always want to be seen to be right and they are like that with most of the Travellers.' Despite the rigidity of the school curriculum and the lack of resources, there were a number of targeted strategies available in the school that in theory offered the prospect of support and greater inclusivity.

Reference to Gypsy culture in the curriculum was scant. The most visible feature of Gypsy and Traveller culture was a display cabinet that a classroom assistant employed by the Traveller Education Service made with a small number of Gypsy students. The display, with models of bow-top wagons, pictures of horses and pieces of Crown Derby china, was now tatty with age and neglect. The cabinet stood in the school reception but, significantly, after the refurbishment of the reception, the cabinet was left neglected in a small storeroom, with no attempt being made to restore the cabinet to its former glory or replace it with a new exhibition of Gypsy and Traveller culture. A long-standing teacher, who was sympathetic to the Gypsies, commented:

> Well, I don't think we're flexible enough for many of our groups
> of children in school. I'm sure a lot more could be done to raise
> the status of Traveller children as a group and to give them an

identity. From time to time you feel things have moved on and various work has come in bits but it never gets to a pitch where it is significant as I dream it might be. There will be some sort of public demonstration of their culture and the Traveller Education Service will come in and do some lessons with some groups in history and lessons like that, it just seems to be scratching the surface always, it's better than nothing at all but it's probably not as comprehensive as it should be. I guess it's down to the school to do more and not expect the Traveller Education Service to do everything.

Despite this limited recognition of Gypsy culture, South Forest School had been praised in its most recent Ofsted report for celebrating the diversity that existed within the school and examples such as Black History Month and the Gypsy cabinet exhibition were cited. Ofsted were clearly happy to accept tokenistic gestures as commitment to diversity. A more in-depth and nuanced analysis of the progress that minority groups were making in the school might have indicated that some minorities did not feel cherished and valued. An approach directed at institutional racism that looked at the wider curriculum and power structures in the school, and the impact of these on achievement and integration, might have concluded that an exam-based and academic curriculum, heavily based on formal teaching, disadvantaged some minorities such as sections of the Gypsy community.

## Targeted support

Two-thirds of the Gypsy students in South Forest School were classified as having special educational needs (SEN) and were therefore eligible for additional learning support. A key component of effective SEN support is to ensure differentiation and personalized work, increasing the possibility for a student to experience success, which in turn can have a positive effect on a student's self-esteem, motivation and behaviour (Welsh and Williams, 2005). Again, though, there was an issue of resources. The coordinator for SEN in the school noted:

The main thing when you are talking about resources is staff. We haven't got enough people to be able to provide that sort of service [innovative and individually designed learning programmes] for a large number of kids. We've got very few teaching assistants and teachers in the unit, so when you talk about resources, the thing we need more is people.

One incident that offered insights into the level of flexibility in the curriculum and the degree of educational inclusion concerned the post of Gypsy Bridge Worker. This was a position designed by South Forest Council, which utilized a government grant for tackling antisocial behaviour and criminality among youth by establishing community worker posts for a number of 'at risk' communities, including Gypsies, in the South Forest area. The community workers were to build better links between home and school, and also find activities and courses to engage non-attenders. However, friction soon emerged between the post-holder, Sue Butler, and the school management. Sue, although not from the Gypsy community, had a background of involvement in Gypsy and Traveller arts projects and wanted to focus on relationship-building with the Gypsies in the South Forest area. Once trust had been established, she would proceed to design initiatives for disaffected Gypsy students.

South Forest School became impatient when few measurable goals had been achieved after three months. The school management team were vociferous in demanding that the post-holder should contribute more directly to initiatives to persuade the Gypsy students to return to school and give assistance within the school to those students who needed support. This created tension, as Sue Butler felt that the school was being short-sighted, focusing on immediate concerns such as improving attendance without seeking to explore the more fundamental reasons for Gypsy students' disaffection. Eventually she resigned. She told me about her reasons:

> I resigned for a number of reasons, some to do with a mismatch between what I thought I was and should be doing and what they [the school] wanted. The job title, 'Gypsy Bridge Worker', was a bit of a euphemism. What they actually wanted was someone who would go round and persuade kids back into school. I would have liked to work in a broader way. Also, if there are reasons why they [Gypsy students] didn't attend, then the school shouldn't assume that it's because the Travellers are somehow amiss, but maybe the school needs to look to itself.

The catalyst for her resignation had been the school's demand for a work plan with specific targets. Commenting on this and on the resignation, Steve Cartwright, the head teacher, declared:

> She [Sue] never got going. I assumed something had gone wrong on the Traveller site. I had a meeting with her and she showed me a load of photos and I suggested we get the teenagers who were

not attending into literacy classes where they could also do some photography with her. I just wanted them engaged in something. I don't have low expectations, it's just better than doing nothing. She wouldn't tell us where she was, and weeks would fly by and you would never see her. Then it was suggested that she produce a work plan, which wasn't asking too much. She wasn't coming under huge pressure, but she just left.

It may have been that the school had failed to grasp the importance of developing relationships with the Gypsy community and designing a programme that reflected their needs and aspirations. Instead, a work programme was to be imposed that fitted the school's conception of the situation. The rigidity of the curriculum and the pressures that schools are under to see quantifiable outcomes for projects at an early stage appeared to have hamstrung an initiative that could have increased the Gypsies' educational participation. The desire to work in a broad and flexible manner, as espoused by Sue Butler, and a desire by the school to see quantifiable results as quickly as possible, leading to increased formal participation in school, were not always reconcilable and the initiative floundered because of the mutual mistrust and tension that arose from these two approaches. With regard to the non-attenders that the Gypsy Bridge Worker post had focused on, it was resolved that a special class solely for Gypsy non-attenders would be established, which they would attend in the mornings only. It was hoped that the class would help the non-attenders adjust to school life and reintegrate. A TES teacher who worked in an authority near to South Forest, and who had worked with Gypsies and Travellers since the late 1970s, rationalized the logic of establishing such a special class:

> I remember in the early days going on sites and doing educational activities with young Travellers, but we fought hard to get them into schools. However, when you look at sites like South Forest where there has been a complete rupture in relations between the school and community, there's somehow a need in some cases to go back to 1970s solutions, which involves some activity outside of the mainstream.

Initially the special classes were well attended but the teaching was led by two local authority teachers from outside the school who were SEN specialists but who had no experience of Gypsy students. The teachers served up learning experiences that were similar to those to be found in the mainstream curriculum and had limited scope for creativity. The teachers were also unable to foster a strong discipline code. The classes unravelled, leading to serious discipline incidents and then a reversion to non-attendance by the students. A number of teachers reached the conclusion that the local authority had directed the appointed teachers to this particular project as they were their weaker staff members who were 'surplus to requirements' and could be spared for a project that was deemed to have limited prospects of success. If Sue Butler had remained in post and had been involved in the project, the chances of success might have been greater, given the specialist knowledge she could have brought to the enterprise.

Traveller Education Services are sections of the Local Education Authority that give support to Gypsy and Traveller students in accessing education, but that also give strategic advice and guidance to schools. A key component in enabling a TES to fulfil its role is to develop positive relationships with Gypsy and Traveller parents. Given the polarized relations between some schools and Gypsy and Traveller parents, these relationships could be brought under strain as either side in a dispute tried to draw the TES into supporting its particular grievance. This had been the fate of the South Forest TES at South Forest School. Gypsy parents were angered because they felt that the TES was siding with the school in the dispute. In turn, the school failed to appreciate the strategic role of the service and felt that it should be more proactive and 'hands on' in increasing Gypsy student participation in school rather than expecting the school to take the initiative. A report for the Department for Education and Skills conducted several years after my observation suggested that such tensions were common (Ivatts, 2005). The school failed to recognize the limited resources of the TES – a small staff team had to support many schools in the area and its primary role was to give strategic advice that schools should use to guide them. As noted earlier, the school had failed to consider a key piece of advice from the TES, which was to utilize professional mediation services to broker a more positive relationship with the Gypsies.

During my observation I had worked closely with the TES and in the wake of a fight between a Black student and a Gypsy student I was reprimanded by a Gypsy parent:

> Tell me please, I know that school has no control and they let the Blacks do what they want but ours get punished for nothing. It was wrong they expelled [name of student]: he was only standing up against a bully, doing what we have always done in our culture, that is, stand up for each other. Why did you allow

that to happen? Why didn't you stand up to that Mr Cartwright [South Forest head teacher] and say he was wrong?

On the other hand, it appeared that some staff at South Forest School felt hostility towards the TES. I had often sensed a hostile atmosphere when walking into the staffroom with Simon James, the head of the TES. He also acknowledged the existence of this hostility and felt that it was the product of tensions between the school and the site. I noted how few of the staff would enter into conversation with me or Simon and how staff discussions in small groups would sometimes abruptly end when Simon or I entered the staffroom. One of the classroom assistants who transferred from the primary school to the secondary school was a Gypsy living on the South Forest Site. She was entitled to sit in the staffroom, but this caused anxiety from staff who were concerned she might overhear comments by staff about Gypsy students. The view of the TES was that this would only be a problem if improper comments were being made about Gypsy students. The concern of staff on this matter may have reflected the fact that many negative comments were being made in the staffroom about the Gypsies.

A lack of resources and in some cases poor planning and understanding by the school, coupled with a formal curriculum, appeared to hamper many of the measures available to support Gypsy students and to increase their educational inclusion. Instead, many Gypsy students seemed to be consigned to learning experiences that failed to inspire them or address their needs, leading to disruption in class and non-attendance. The case study, 'Anatomy of a furore', later in this chapter, provides insights into how these factors accentuated educational exclusion.

## Student subculture

One teacher at South Forest School noted with reference to a male Gypsy student who was part of the resister subgroup:

> He cooperates in school only on his own terms and when he chooses. He is threatening to teachers and refuses to follow instructions. He frequently truants from lessons. He makes racist comments and threats to Black members of his tutor group. He fails to respond to the report system. He is disengaged from the education process. He has stated that it is his intention to leave in Year 9 and therefore fails to see the point in cooperating.

Such traits can be classified as revealing school subculture behaviour on the part of this student. From the 1970s a series of ethnographic studies appeared that claimed to have captured a more complex picture of school experiences in which student subcultures were able to articulate opposition and resistance. Student subcultures are characterized as involving intensive interaction within the group, a common situation taking the form of a role or problem, and shared goals and values (a group perspective). Probably the most influential student subculture study is Willis's study of working-class youth. He argues that, disillusioned with an academic curriculum and contemptuous of schools' claims to be a meritocracy, the 'lads', as he terms the alienated working-class youth, developed coping mechanisms to manage their educational alienation that involved ascribing status to work-avoidance strategies and that sought to relieve the monotony of school life by seeking opportunities to have a 'laugh' (Willis, 1977).

Several studies of student subcultures have focused on race (Majors and Billson, 1992; Gillborn, 1990; Sewell, 1997). Majors and Billson (1992) claim that the Black youth they studied responded to the racism they endured in society and school by developing a 'cool pose', a strategy of opposition to school. This strategy enabled the alienated students to regain the status and self-esteem that had been eroded by low teacher expectations and racism and to show they were strong and proud and capable of survival despite the low status they were accorded by society. These researchers depict their subjects as displaying accentuated forms of masculinity, suggesting that gendered behaviour is socially constructed. This 'hypermasculinity' emphasized toughness, ridiculed the masculinity of those who conformed by associating schoolwork with femininity, and resulted in aggressive behaviour and conflict with staff.

Subculture resistance theories suggest that such masculinity is atavistically regenerating traditional cultural traits, such as reactionary white working-class notions of manhood and African traditions of displaying masculinity through dance, initiation rituals and warrior cults (Majors *et al.*, 1994). A connection therefore exists between the formation of subcultures and their parent culture (Woods and Hammersley, 1993). Subculture formation can be viewed as a response to racism or economic exploitation and, in an educational context, to other forms of oppression such as 'labelling', where students are marked out as 'deviants' and 'outsiders' (Gillborn, 1990). Such theories contrast to the tendency to view subculture students through a deficit model that pathologizes such students. This culturalist perspective suggests that social behaviour is to be understood in terms of a perceived deviant culture and that ethnicity and not society is the problem (Majors and Billson, 1992).

The group of students I called the resisters were a student subculture with a sense of identity that was strengthened by perceptions of hostile forces that included the school, authority and other ethnic groups. Group identity was solidified by a strong honour code (symbolic capital – see Chapter 3) that prompted resistance to perceived unfair treatment by fellow students and even staff. Such a strategy prompted a strong degree of hypermasculinity on the part of the resisters. In Gypsy culture, fighting is a major signifier of masculinity that can translate as prestige and status (Levinson and Sparkes, 2003). As will be seen in the case study 'Anatomy of a furore', female Gypsy students also ascribed to this honour code and were willing to use force. Studies of school student subcultures have tended to portray them as the preserve of male students. Such studies reaffirm the perception of female students as more passive or as constructing less overt resistance, such as 'accommodation within resistance' where females strive to achieve academic success but do not fully subscribe to or accept the ethos of the school (Mirza, 1992). There has been an androcentric tendency in some accounts of Gypsy and Traveller students' experiences that has not paid sufficient attention to gender issues and, where it has, has recorded rigid gender roles and patriarchy and failed to consider if these have undergone adaptation. The masculinized response of the female resisters at South Forest School therefore provides important new insights.

In my interviews with Gypsy resister students, I recorded a large number of negative comments about other ethnic minority students: 'Black people smell, they put all that cream on them. To be honest they think they own the school.' Another student stated: 'I wouldn't take Black boys who are friends down to the site because they would probably be called names and get beaten up. … My mum, she ain't being racist or nothing, but she thinks they are taking over this country. We were here before anyone else was.' Some of the Gypsy students' xenophobia reflected growing racial tensions in South Forest, which had witnessed the growth of Black and white gangs that fought each other on race lines. These tensions and hostilities are illustrated in the case study.

## Case study: Anatomy of a furore

When I arrived at South Forest School in spring 2003, there had been two major disturbances within the school in the previous three years. These had taken on a mythical status and were often referred to by the staff when talking about the Gypsies. Both disturbances were manifestations of the tensions that existed in relationships between the Gypsies and the school and the wider community. The disturbances, often referred to by the different parties as the 'riots', occurred in 2000 and 2001. Simon James, the head of South Forest TES, felt that the Gypsies were wrongly blamed for the first 'riot'. In 2000 there had been a fight in the school and as a consequence hundreds of students refused to return to their lessons and ran amok in the school. The Gypsies were a prominent group that got carried away and joined in the melee. The Gypsies were brought into prominence in this incident by the fact that one Gypsy parent (Ethel Burrage, wife of Tom who featured in Chapter 3) came into the school, rounded up many of the Gypsy students and marched them out of the school. This act was no doubt viewed as a further humiliation to the authority of the school.

A year later, in 2001, a fight broke out; allegedly Bridget Burrage (daughter of Tom and Ethel), a Year-9 student, had goaded a Somali boy. The boy had retaliated and headbutted Bridget, leaving her with a bleeding nose. Apparently Bridget threw a bin and stool across the room and then moved from class to class, collecting a large number of Gypsy students, who congregated in a group in the playground. Bridget contacted her parents by mobile phone about the incident and the parents came into the school reception. The distraught parents argued with the head teacher, Steve Cartwright, in reception. Ethel Burrage then repeated the action she took in 2000 and proceeded into the school playground, collected many of the Gypsy students and took them out of the school. In the tail of this were a large group of inquisitive non-Gypsy students, who took advantage of an opportunity to create further mayhem. For the second time Mrs Burrage had shown a lack of faith and confidence in the school and for a second time had withdrawn the Gypsy students en masse from the school, an act that again seriously challenged the authority of the school.

The boy who was involved in the clash was excluded for two days but many of the Gypsies felt this was an insufficient punishment. The conflict between the Somalis and Gypsies continued after this, as some of the Gypsy students sought revenge, in particular against the boy who had hit Bridget. Two days after the fight, when this boy returned to school, he was attacked by a boy from the South Forest Traveller Site.

Conflict also took place outside the school. Several parents on the South Forest Site informed me that one day the Gypsy teenagers from the site had to run home as a gang of Somalis chased them from the school. For a long time after the second disturbance many of the Gypsy students stayed away from school. A long-standing and sympathetic member of staff noted the boycott:

> There was a dramatic impact: pretty much all the Gypsies [from
> the site] withdrew for several months ... en masse for some time.
> Several months later a few filtered back. It was a very difficult
> time: there was a complete breakdown in relations between the
> Traveller community and the school. Lots of effort was put into
> making links but it took a long time, but I think things have got
> back to an even keel, but I think there is still a time issue. They
> do seem to have largely let it go, but I don't think all the parents
> are happy about the way their children are dealt with in school.

The Gypsies on the site believed that the disturbance in 2001 confirmed
many of their anxieties about the school. In their opinion, the school did
not offer a safe environment and newcomers such as the Somalis received
favourable treatment. The school was deemed to be prejudiced against
Gypsies. The head teacher was considered to have been unfairly lax with
the Somali boy and merely excluded him for a matter of days, while Bridget,
who they perceived as the victim, was severely reprimanded by being
excluded for four weeks. It is in this context that Simon James from the
TES had suggested using the local authority mediation service to initiate
dialogue and greater understanding. The mediation service was enthusiastic
about taking on such a role. The head teacher chose not to take up this offer.
In the opinion of the TES this was because he was adamant that the problem
lay with the Gypsies and it was merely a matter of the 'Gypsies playing by
the rules'.

The notion that time may have healed these tensions was rudely
shattered in autumn 2003. The school term had started in what the
management no doubt considered to be a buoyant mood. For some time the
school had been under threat from the local authority's academy proposal.
The talks about the future of the school were now reaching a critical stage
but the school management team was encouraged by the improved GCSE
results (General Certificate of Secondary Education, taken at the age of 16),
which they believed would strengthen their campaign. In the previous year,
13 per cent of students had achieved five GCSEs at grades A to C; this year,
it had been 25 per cent. At this time the government target for 'challenging
schools' was 20 per cent. In the staff meeting at the start of the academic
year, the head teacher reiterated his intention to oppose the local authority's
plans for the school and said:

> I want to fight the local authority's proposal; that takes strength
> and determination but I need all my staff behind me and more

positive publicity building upon our GCSE results as it will be crucial during this time to save the school.

The buoyant mood of the school management was to be severely dented, for a serious incident was to occur, which was comparable to the major disturbances that had taken place in previous years. One of the female Gypsy students got into a fight with a Black African-Caribbean female student, which was stopped by the intervention of the head teacher. The head teacher made the two girls agree to end their differences and apologize. The head teacher thought that this would resolve the matter. However, that day, as school finished, a major fight took place outside the school. A group of Gypsies (composed mainly of those not attending school) waited outside the school. They had received a mobile phone call telling them about the fight in the school and they were there to provide support. The school secretary was alerted to the perceived danger and called via the public address system for all male members of staff to go to the bus stop where the group from the site was waiting. This was a serious mistake as the school was finishing for the day and hundreds of students were alerted to the disturbance and, rather than going home, they decided to stay around in order to watch the fracas.

The head teacher and several members of staff demanded that the group go home but these entreaties were ignored and one of the female Gypsy students (sister of the girl involved in the scuffle in the school) attacked the Black student involved in the earlier incident. This fight took place in front of the management team. The next day the head teacher convened a special staff meeting and, according to Simon James who heard reports of what happened, some of the staff said that they were afraid of the Gypsy students. Simon James was not invited to this meeting and was very concerned that the school did not contact him immediately to inform him about the incident. He found out two days later.

The following Monday I came into the school. The Gypsy parents of the children involved in the clash, came into school to meet the head teacher. Simon James and I were also invited to the meeting. The parents accepted the permanent exclusion of several of the children. I sensed that they were not entirely sorry; in fact, one parent said it would have been more of a punishment to make their child attend, a statement that reflected the low regard she had for the school and the dire state of the relationship between the site and the school. However, the Black student involved in the initial scuffle went unpunished. The head teacher said that he did not feel a need to punish this student as she had apologized for her initial misdemeanours. However, the assembled parents accused the head teacher of double standards. The whole episode was a rerun of previous clashes. In response, the head teacher stated that he had a good track record on equal opportunities, implying that the school was not at fault. The conversation went around in circles, with both sides repeating the same points until one of the parents appeared to lose her patience and left the room in protest. The meeting ended, and the head teacher was distressed and shaken. Simon James still felt that the school was failing to listen to the Gypsies.

Simon and I visited the site. We met the Gypsy student involved in the fight outside the school and asked her why she had hit the Black student. She responded that the Black girl had attacked her sister and she was only standing up for her sister. Again, a 'you attack us and we'll attack you' mentality was being demonstrated. We also visited the parents, who informed us that there were rumours that the Black student's friends were planning to attack Gypsy students outside the school. Again, as with the case with the Somalis, it seemed as if the stage was being set for a long period of tension and possible feuding between rival groups. A further claim by one parent was clearly untrue. She said there was a rumour in circulation that the Black female student who was attacked had been pregnant and had lost her baby in the fight and this was why the Black students were so eager for revenge. Such was the fear that the Gypsies on the site felt of the wider community and groups on the estate that the Gypsies again were ready to believe the worst, including unfounded rumours, and felt under siege.

At the heart of the tensions may have been a perception that the Gypsies' culture was continually being hemmed in by external forces, and that they were being persecuted. In spite of the fact that there had been no serious disturbances for two years, the fundamental problems in the relationship between the school and the Traveller site still existed. The root of these problems is complex and forms part of a matrix of exclusion involving the strained relations with the school and factors beyond the boundaries of school life that predated the onset of problems between the school and the site.

## Conclusion

At South Forest School, the management's failure to foster a 'preventative approach' and promote dialogue, mediation and innovative anti-racist measures contributed to the difficult relations within the school. A policy of punitive sanctions and negative labelling led to a perception by the Gypsies that there was not a climate of justice in the school, a notion that can do much to fuel student resistance (Docking, 1989). Student subcultures can be a reaction to an authoritarian management approach, racism and negative labelling (Hargreaves, 1982). South Forest School had adopted a 'crisis management' approach, one that was reactionary and located the problem in the child. If the school had moved away from its ethnocentrism and instead adopted intercultural dialogue, it might have come to realize that the values and practices that suit one culture may not work well for another. More to the point, the school might have concluded that the behaviour of the Gypsies and Travellers involved in the school counterculture, which the head teacher and staff viewed as repugnant, was in fact a 'cry for help', was fuelled by considerable vulnerability and insecurity on the part of the students and was a product of exclusion and racism.

In defence of the school, under-resourced and serving an area characterized by high levels of social exclusion, it was not in a good position to introduce an ambitious and complex piece of legislation like the amended Race Relations Act of 2000, which stipulated that schools should develop action plans to counter racism and discrimination and foster good community relations. However, more resources coupled with an action plan that had been carefully negotiated with staff and ethnic minority communities could have had an important impact on the work of the school in tackling disadvantage and discrimination, and improving community relations. The Race Relations Act as amended had come into force only one year prior to my fieldwork and many schools and institutions experienced difficulty in effectively implementing its provisions (Runnymede Trust, 2003). Furthermore, the limitations of the national curriculum and resources gave the school limited room for manoeuvre.

# Chapter 5

# Identity, exclusion and change

Chapters 3 and 4 described how the South Forest Gypsies (adults and adolescents) had adopted divergent life strategies and responses to school. Many of the Gypsies observed fell into two broad groups: resister and mainstreamer. This chapter explores in greater depth and theorizes the strategies adopted by the resisters, focusing on the South Forest Traveller Site.

## Identity and symbolic capital

> A sense of common origin, of common beliefs and of a common feeling of survival – in brief a 'common cause' has been important in uniting people.
>
> (De Vos, 1995: 15)

The factors identified by De Vos played a role in the formation of group identity on the South Forest Traveller Site. As this chapter will show, other factors beyond the rituals and symbols of culture contributed to the formation of group identity. Dramatic changes had taken place for many Gypsies across the country: in the case of the South Forest Gypsies, moving within 50 years from living a truly nomadic life to living in houses on a large, modern housing estate or having pitches on the highly regulated local authority site. These major changes had a great impact on traditional lifestyles and created new environmental and cultural influences. The Gypsies on the South Forest Site had sought to diminish the influences of these external factors by maintaining, as far as possible, a cultural distance between their lives and those of the wider community. For many, being a Gypsy was a primary identity. A factor that fuelled distancing was resentment. As discussed in Chapter 4 this resentment, which was a form of cultural trauma, had been shaped by the dramatic changes imposed upon them against their will and the exclusion that they still endured, and took the form of hostility towards institutions such as school as well as a fear and distrust of the wider community.

The resisters believed that distancing strategies and minimal interaction with those outside the group would prevent cultural dilution. Douglas (1966) notes how some cultures have divided society into sacred and profane, and have developed taboo and avoidance rules to navigate and define these distinctions. Douglas argues that such rules should be viewed as a statement about wider society and as unique assertions by groups as to who they are. In other words, identity is relational and difference is established by symbolic marking in relation to others. Okely (1983, and also see Chapter 1) shows how, through elaborate hygiene rituals, Gypsies perceived non-Gypsies who did not follow these rules as being polluted and as posing a threat. It is debatable how stringently these rules are now observed among Gypsies. However, it can be argued that among groups such as the resisters a new set of fears and taboos had emerged that needed to be avoided and observed, respectively.

Wider society was held to pose danger because of its moral code. The elder Gypsies on the South Forest Site frequently castigated the settled community on the estate for their perceived high levels of criminality, as well as their immorality in the form of drug abuse and promiscuity. These fears in part accounted for, or were used to justify, non-attendance at school, where it was thought that young Gypsies were vulnerable to possible moral contagion from their corrupt school peers. That Gypsies on the South Forest Estate compared their moral probity to the excesses they believed were evident in the school and on the estate, together with their intense sense of social honour, could be viewed as a compensatory mechanism for the extreme levels of exclusion that they endured.

Gypsies placed a strong emphasis on symbolic capital (prestige and honour; see Chapter 4). Symbolic capital could be maximized by conforming to the 'Gypsy way', a set of dispositions that for group members comprised their perception of what it was to be a Gypsy. An important component of this sense of prestige and honour was to defend the group and oneself from challenge and threat. Failure to offer defence could lead to the loss of public face and was deemed to create a dangerous situation where others could try to take advantage of the injured party. Therefore, family and group honour had to be fiercely defended. There are cases where the adversary also adheres to such an honour code or is in a position where it is dangerous to be perceived as weak. As a consequence, disputes in societies where symbolic capital is prized can be intense and protracted (Kriesberg, 2003). Hence, conflicts within the Gypsy community have been known to take the form of vendettas, span generations and encompass wide extended family networks. Acton *et al.* describe the honour code among English Gypsies/Romanichals:

> In such a system individuals are responsible for asserting their own rights and the rights of family dependents who are weaker than they are, or friends or kin who are unjustly outnumbered. ...

> Not to stand up personally for one's rights or those of a weaker
> dependant if one has been wronged is to be shamed, 'ladged' in
> English Romani.
>
> (Acton et al., 1997: 145)

Two of the principal antagonists for the Gypsies on the South Forest
Site were the school and the recently arrived Somali community, who, as
refugees, had been placed in social housing on the South Forest Estate. It is
ironic that the Somalis shared many of the traits of the Gypsies. A Somali
community worker who worked with the Somali teenagers in South Forest
told me that the Somalis, like the Gypsies, had a strong sense of pride and
would not countenance making concessions to those with whom they were
engaged in a dispute. Their strong honour code was demonstrated when
they grouped together and fought vigorously to defend group honour. This
was why the clash between the Somalis and the Gypsies had been so intense
and protracted. (See the section 'Symbolic capital and inter-ethnic conflict',
in this chapter.)

Symbolic capital reinforced group formation: so as to protect and
maintain group honour the Gypsy students termed resisters needed to gang
together. 'We all stick up for each other. The Travellers stick together, they
fight together and they run together', exclaimed one of the adolescents
living on the South Forest Site. Grouping also provided a means of self-help
to fend off the dangers of a hostile world. As one female Gypsy student
informed me, 'If one of us gets fighting with someone, then we're all up to
the school. We all stick up for each other.' I reasoned with this student about
the logic of confrontation and asked whether she ever contemplated not
seeking revenge but she poured scorn on such a notion: 'You must be soft,
mate; if I did that people would think I was soft and all, and walk all over
me. If anyone gives me a hard time, they'll get this [clenched fist] in the face.'
For this student, belligerence was a clear feature of group identity but also
a response to generations of exclusion and discrimination:

> In olden times, people called us names, they didn't like us and
> now we're standing up to them. ... Travellers act like their parents
> and are strong in arguments, they don't like losing and want to
> come out on top, and they want people to know that so they will
> not take them on.

The alternative to retaliation was not to be countenanced. A Gypsy
adolescent from the site told me that one day he had gone to the shops,
and a group of Somali boys laughed at him, which led to a scuffle. I asked

him why he hadn't ignored this act. The teenager replied: 'If I did that then I would have them on my back all the time.' The outcome of his act of retaliation, however, was that a gang of Somalis came to the site in turn, seeking their revenge.

In demonstrating resentment and the maintenance of symbolic capital, a section of Gypsy and Traveller students, like their marginalized counterparts in the Kosovan, Somali and Vietnamese communities, had come together in subcultures that ritualistically played out expressions of anger. With reference to such groups, a subculture is an effort to resolve collectively experienced problems that generate a form of collective identity from which an individual identity can be achieved (Brod and Kaufman, 1994).

As a student subculture, the resisters had created a set of perceptions and rituals that shaped their interactions with their peers and the school authorities. Haas and Shaffir (1982) argue that a dramaturgical approach can help in understanding human behaviour; conduct can be viewed as a performance in which the script has to be enacted in such a way as to make the performance of a role credible to the audience (see also Goffman, 1959 and the discussion in Chapter 1). Such an approach can offer important insights into the nature of protracted disputes between marginalized groups and authority. In their portrayal of Black relations in the St Pauls riot in Bristol in 1980, Joshua *et al.* (1983) argue that the rioting demonstrated a shared understanding of racism that expressed itself in a violent form. Turner (1967) described the oppositionality of the Ndemu in Zambia as a 'social drama'. These crisis situations had regular and predictable features. Symbols and rituals strengthen the consciousness of a community and to be effective they have to be invoked and repeated at regular intervals (Woodward, 2000).

Thus, the conflicts and resulting actions from the resisters had an almost formulaic and repetitive quality in terms of how situations were interpreted and how they, as individuals or as a group, decided to respond. The resisters concluded that school 'had it in for them' and that the prejudice towards them shaped the treatment they were accorded, treatment that they classified as unfair and that they felt had to be questioned and challenged for the sake of their 'honour'. These symbolic displays created a sense of camaraderie and solidarity among the resisters. The resisters' conflicts had predictable patterns and starting points and conclusions.

## Symbolic capital and school

The resisters felt that school was unfair and that it unfairly punished Gypsy students. It may even have become a locus for the resentment they felt at generations of exclusion: here was an agent of authority that, unlike many of the other entities they felt were responsible for their exclusion, they could clearly identify and with which they were in frequent contact. Following the second serious disturbance in the school, the Gypsy students, with the support of their parents, boycotted the school for a considerable period of time (see Chapter 4). Although not all of the resisters were directly affected by this incident, they felt that the female Gypsy involved in the classroom fight with a Somali boy had been unfairly dealt with by the school because she was suspended for defending herself against what they considered to be a racist attack. Group honour dictated that they should show solidarity with the girl and express their disapproval of the school's action by not attending school. Adams *et al.* (1975) noted how Gypsy kin group solidarity is especially apparent in disputes or crises, and this was clearly still the case 30 years later.

The Gypsies' protracted dispute with the school could be considered a feud. This feud may not have been without foundation in terms of their perception of ill-treatment, given the very high exclusion rate. Many researchers have found that if students believe school is treating them unfairly, then they may have trouble in accepting school rules (Gibson, 1988). As discussed in Chapter 4, the school management at South Forest School considered the Gypsies from the site to be particularly troublesome, a factor that in their opinion was a threat to their authority and the efficient running of the school. The TES was concerned that the school management team appeared to assign all the blame for the conflicts to the Gypsies by ascribing their misbehaviour to their perceived racism. It was interesting to note that, on a number of occasions where the head teacher had covered lessons or intervened in a conflict situation, the Gypsy students had failed to yield to his authority. Was this a factor that explained the poor behaviour of the Gypsy students, not just with the school management team, but with some members of staff? Did the Gypsy students perceive such staff to be hostile, and consequently offer resistance? One South Forest schoolteacher, who worked in the Pupil Support Unit stated:

> Sometimes kids are coming here and saying, 'all I did was to walk into the classroom and this or that happened.' Now, quite often you can tell it is their fault, but there are times when teachers are at fault: teachers are human beings and they are going to take a dislike to students; it shouldn't happen but it does. All it takes is for that kid to do something small, which if some other kid did you might act in a different way, but if you have had a history of

trouble with them then that will be it and you will say, 'get out'.
There is six of one and half a dozen of the other: it's not always
the kids: there are times when teachers gang up and don't give
kids a chance.

## Symbolic capital and inter-ethnic conflict

A South Forest School staff member, who had taught at the School for 25
years, believed that the community felt they were getting a 'raw deal' and
were tired of being 'bottom of the pile'. This had exacerbated racial tensions:

> I think there has been a shift in recent years, with a lot of children
> coming from abroad, and I think there's been a lot of conflict
> between Travellers and some of the other ethnic groups, and I
> think that's about power basically, about who's going to be 'top
> dog' or 'second in the pecking order' and who's going to be
> 'bottom of the pile'.

'Invidious comparison' is where a group is of the opinion that an 'out
group' is being afforded greater privilege without having greater worth. The
perception of disparate privilege often has little foundation (Rubin *et al.*,
1994). The perception the Gypsies had that the Somalis and other asylum
seekers were being privileged was a major factor in the maintenance of their
conflict. Up until the early 1970s the estate had been predominantly white
working class but now there was a large Black and Indian community. Recent
years had also seen the arrival of relatively large numbers of asylum seekers,
mainly from Kosovo, Somalia and Vietnam. The resentment towards these
other ethnic groups was intense on the site, as the perception was that they
were getting treated better than the Gypsies, who felt that as they had been
there longer they should, to quote one Gypsy adult, be at the 'front of the
queue, not the back'. There was also anger at the violence that the Gypsies
believed was directed towards them from these minorities. These responses
are similar to those recorded by Hewitt (2005) in the borough of Greenwich
around the time of the murder of Stephen Lawrence in 1993: the white
working class were aggrieved at their perceived loss of privilege to ethnic
minorities, which in their opinion had disadvantaged them, giving rise to
racist extremism. In his study of multiracial urban environments, Back notes
white working-class racism and comments:

> Thus racist reactions identified in the adult population have to be
> viewed in terms of how working class people react to and make
> meaningful sense of their economic and social situation, racism

became a way of explaining the declining housing conditions by correlating these changes with the presence of 'black' and 'yellow' people.

(Back, 1996: 97)

These conclusions could also explain the cause of the resisters' racism towards other minorities. These factors motivated what some outsiders believed to be the racism of the Gypsies on the site. Indeed, many of the attitudes they expressed towards other ethnic groups were racist, but some in the school used this as a means of dismissing them out of hand. Few appreciated that this racism and scapegoating was a product of their marginalization, reflected in the spatial and racial exclusion they endured, which was steadily eroding their traditional lifestyle. It is not uncommon for marginalized groups to blame other similar groups for their misfortunes, because they are more apparent and identifiable targets than policymakers and structural factors, which might otherwise be held to account (Stark, 1994).

The resisters used their cultural identity as the building blocks to mount resistance to the numerous enemies they perceived as being set against them. The resisters became ultra-conservative in their cultural ideals, according higher status and esteem to adherence to traditional Gypsy lifestyles and deriding those, such as the mainstreamers, who embraced change and adaptation. 'Reactive ethnicity' is a tendency for ethnic groups to construct ethnicity as a defence against racism and discrimination. Ballard and Ballard (1977) note how second-generation Sikhs sought to strike compromises with British society but were stung into increased pride in their ethnicity because of racism. Similar developments have been noted in the African-Caribbean community (Pilkington, 2003). Reactive ethnicity can intensify perceptions of group boundaries, providing opportunities to affirm identities and group loyalties (Rubin *et al.*, 1994). It can thus increase the chance of inter-ethnic conflict. As I will argue in the following sections of this chapter, this cultural strategy could therefore be counterproductive.

The intensity of the conflict between the Somalis and the Gypsies and Travellers was born out of the striking similarities between the two groups. The violent disintegration of Somali society had caused cultural trauma, which the Gypsy community had also experienced. Somali culture, also like that of the Gypsies and Travellers, was based on clan traditions and nomadism. Together with Islam, this was a central foundation of Somali culture and habitus. Within Somali culture there is also a prevailing sense of insecurity and hegemonic masculinity. Keynan states:

These characteristics, particularly, the perception of threat, have become deeply embedded in the fabric of the Somali equation [culture]. As a result Somali society's core traditions have become impregnated with a kind of siege mentality and primeval quest for survival, with men assuming the roles of protectors and providers. This in turn has led to the emergence of a pattern of socialisation that glorifies and rewards aggressiveness, bravery, courage, strength and toughness, traits associated with the macho role.

(Keynan, 2000: 190)

Keynan proceeds to argue that the culture of conflict underlying the Somali clan system can be attributed to the centrality of a feud culture. The similarities between the Somalis and Gypsies at South Forest intensified and prolonged their feud.

## Gender and conflict

As discussed in Chapter 4, from the 1970s onwards a series of ethnographic studies captured a more complex picture of school experiences, in which student subcultures were able to articulate opposition and resistance to regain status and self-esteem. These researchers described their subjects as displaying accentuated forms of masculinity, referred to as 'hypermasculinity'. Bourdieu (1995) may be justified in describing masculinity as one of the last refuges of the identity of the dominated classes. For the resisters, masculinity provided a means by which discontents could be articulated.

Membership of the resisters' subculture at South Forest School was not confined to male Gypsy students; neither was challenging behaviour, as girls were not only involved in conflicts but also orchestrated and led some serious challenges in the school. The female resisters often did not have the attainment and literacy levels or cultural capital to acculturate as the girls in the mainstreamers group were able to. Most of the female mainstreamers lived in housing and their parents were employed in the waged economy. These factors may have meant they were more embedded in mainstream culture and prepared to 'buy in' to the ethos of school.

Mirza (1992) notes the importance of parental views and gender in her study *Young, Female and Black*, which seeks to explain why Black female students achieve relatively good attainment rates compared with their Black male and working-class peers. Mirza notes the importance of valuing the economic role of the female wage-earner in the Black family, which helps to promote young Black female aspirations. Unlike their Black male counterparts, Black girls were more likely to adopt passive forms of resistance to teachers' racism, such as not taking up particular subjects if they did not feel at ease with staff, as a short-term coping strategy, while at the same time striving for longer-term educational goals and academic success. Mirza (1997) labels this 'resistance in accommodation', a strategy that allows female students indirectly to subvert oppressive structures of authority and racist expectations by achieving academic success and opening up transformative possibilities. As with the students in Mirza's study, the female mainstreamers in South Forest were more likely to adopt passive modes of resistance such as wearing large jewellery, which although popular among Gypsy students infringed school regulations. In general, though, the mainstreamers subscribed to the ethos of the school and hoped to secure academic success and reward.

Research has shown that girls are more likely to reach an accommodation with school and boys are more likely to offer challenges to school authority (Askew and Ross, 1988). Furthermore, femininity as constructed in Western culture has historically been characterized by passivity (Foster *et al.*, 1996), whereas males are expected to be more assertive and aggressive (Hare *et al.*, 1995). The female resisters appeared to defy these trends.

Although an established community, the South Forest Gypsies did not feel secure: they had seen their lifestyle increasingly hemmed in and there was a strong sense of collective mistrust that may have influenced the perceptions of the male and female resisters. Other cultural traditions may have had a part to play. Although heavily gendered roles existed on the South Forest Site, with men being the main breadwinners and women staying at home to tend to domestic duties and look after children, the women did not conform strictly to traditional roles. Gypsy and Traveller women have often been left to mediate with the authorities by men, and to represent the community in a broad range of contacts with the settled community, the perception being that women were better placed to take on such roles (Kendall, 1997). This is one factor that explains why the great majority of Gypsy and Traveller campaigners are women. It may also explain why female Gypsies were prominent in orchestrating challenges to the authority and perceived racism of South Forest School.

In Gypsy culture, men are often expected to take a prominent role in the physical challenges that occur in a feud, but it is not unknown for women to also take on such a role and to be actively involved in the conduct of a feud or defence in the face of a challenge, which can involve distancing as well as assertiveness and violence (Griffin, 2008). The Gypsies at South

Forest Site had entered into a feud with South Forest School, a feud that involved males and females. Their sense of solidarity was one factor that motivated them to group together in challenges. Research has shown how Black female students have shown empathy for their Black male peers at the high exclusion rates they have been subjected to by expressing support for their peers and contempt for the perceived racism of the school, articulating their own challenges to school authority (Wright *et al.*, 2000). This solidarity may have been another factor in motivating the female resisters to play a prominent role in the challenges that took place in school.

Writing about student subcultures, Frosh *et al.* (2002) record membership as being mainly male, exalting macho behaviour, violence and sex and being in opposition to academia. However, each subgroup has its own identity shaped by its own set of circumstances and history (Swain, 2005). At South Forest, such was the pressure on Gypsies and sense of isolation that male and female Gypsies came together in a counterculture. This interaction with females was not considered effeminate by the males, neither did it have a sexual dimension: the girls, often referred to as 'cousins', had the status of extended family members, and indeed some were. This collaboration was confined to the school; on the Traveller site roles and behaviour continued to be heavily gendered, supporting the conclusion that gender identity is situational and shifting. The contrast in behaviour of female Gypsies between the school and the site can in part be explained by the influence of community elders (identity managers) on the site, prescribing patterns of behaviour, whereas the school provided a cultural vacuum where the female Gypsies could devise and articulate new forms of identity and expression.

Research has shown that Black student subcultures can be counterproductive for group members. Hypermasculinity, a common feature of these subcultures, can lead to dangerous behaviour and self-harm. A strong machismo can lead to gang activity, violence and deviance but also internal oppression, as reflected in domestic abuse and sexual oppression, in which an exaggerated phallocentricity seeks to find alternative forms of power to compensate for the exclusion Black men suffer at the hands of mainstream society (hooks, 1992). The Gypsies at South Forest demonstrated some of these traits in the maintenance of a feud culture and their inter-ethnic conflict with rival gangs on the estate, such as the Somalis.

In his famous study of a school subculture, Willis (1977) argues that the 'lads' in his study had a partial understanding of capitalism and a realization that society was not a meritocracy, but their rejection of school led them to reproduce their class position by consigning them to low-grade manual labour. The lads' sexism and racism also obscured their understanding of the structural nature of society. Similar arguments could be made for the resisters of South Forest, who believed themselves to be the victims of racism at the hands of school and wider society, but often diverted blame on to other vulnerable minorities, such as the Somalis, as part of a process of scapegoating or 'dual closure', where the excluded marginalize a weaker group in order to access greater resources or power for themselves (Parkin, 1979).

Brod and Kaufman (1994) argue that subculture strategies also lead to the members becoming targets in the school; their defiance makes them stand out and they are deemed to pose a challenge to the authority of the school, which staff members feel needs to be met with punitive sanctions or more vigilant policing within school. Some teachers, frightened by some Black students' overt masculinity, misunderstand the intention of culture-specific behaviour and overreact (Sewell, 1997). This can result in members of a subculture being accorded unequal punishments, which in turn reinforces perceptions of discrimination (Wright *et al.*, 2000). To maintain control of volatile classroom situations, some teaching staff adopt masculine teaching approaches characterized by authoritarianism, formalism and minimal interaction with students, and even use aggressive strategies to impose control and deter potential challenges (Haywood and Mac an Ghaill, 1996). It is claimed that such approaches, by male and female staff, are detrimental when dealing with students exhibiting hypermasculinity, as these students interpret such teaching strategies as an attack on their masculinity that cannot be allowed to pass unchallenged (Majors *et al.*, 1994).

Strained relations between the school and disaffected Gypsy students were clearly evident at South Forest School, and it can be argued that these were a result of the head teacher's masculine management style, which refused to countenance mediation and dialogue with the disaffected Gypsies. Instead, punitive sanctions and exclusion were the favoured tactics to be employed with this minority. Research has noted the central role that head teachers play in determining the tone set in schools for relations with students and parents and as the key arbitrators in disciplinary matters, moulding the disciplinary regime that operates in a school (Wright *et al.*, 2000). The reliance on sanction rather than mediation at South Forest School provoked and inflamed the hypermasculinity of the resisters.

## Change and adaptation
The process of grouping, and the maintenance of the honour code, gave the resisters on the South Forest Site a means of understanding the

marginalization they suffered, and in particular who was to blame and who posed a threat. The strategy offered physical protection and a mechanism that helped maintain boundaries and identity. However, a key question, in the case of Gypsies is whether the creation of cultural enclaves and oppositional and distancing strategies in response to exclusion are the best means to challenge inequality. Another important question is what the alternatives might have been. In the final section of this chapter, I examine what the implications were of alternative life strategies and why the resisters chose not to adopt them.

Developing alternative life strategies and cultural adaptation could be a difficult process, as deviation from perceived collective values and norms could incur sanctions from other group members. One of the residents who lived on the South Forest Site, Lilly Smith, was not a Gypsy herself. She told me that when she first came on to the site as a teenage bride, the Gypsies were shocked by her 'warmness' and by acts such as kissing in public. She told me that her eldest child had suffered terribly on the site because of bullying by the other Gypsy children. Her Gypsy husband felt it was because the child had been raised as a non-Traveller. As a consequence of this, her husband stated that their other children would be raised more like Gypsies. Interestingly, the eldest child had completed his education and was now attending technical college but living with his non-Gypsy uncle and aunt in a house and not on the site. Apparently he felt a sense of resentment towards the site. The other two children seemed to possess what some teaching staff considered were the group traits of Gypsy students on the site. Both boys had a strong sense of Gypsy identity and extremely poor relations with school staff, and could be very challenging. It was the belief of some staff that it was the fact that they were of mixed ethnic parentage that made them accentuate aspects of the group's culture. A desire to fit in with the other disaffected Gypsies was perceived by staff to come at the price of poor attendance, hostility to other ethnic groups and continual conflict with the school authorities.

Minorities are defined by the boundaries they create, and by sanctions and restraints on behaviour outside the group code. Unity and 'imagined community', which divides the world between 'us and them', is maintained and ideologically reproduced by a system of 'border guards' or 'identity managers' that identify people as members or non-members of a specific collectivity, determined by specific cultural codes and styles of dress and behaviour, customs and language. The story of the non-Traveller who married into the community and her mixed-heritage children demonstrates the pressures these cultural border guards can place on nonconformity and the pull towards conformity to group ideals.

The identity managers who were the most resistant to change were not always what they appeared to be. Among the Gypsies at South Forest there seemed to be a hierarchy of status. Some on the site were often described as 'not real Gypsies' because they behaved in a certain way or because one of their parents was a Gorgio. Those who voiced such criticism considered themselves to be 'pure Gypsies' and 'real Gypsies'. One prominent judge of such boundaries was Jim Hadley, a pensioner who lived on the site. In conversations he frequently bemoaned the changes that had taken place and the assaults that Gypsy culture endured from the Gorgio. One day, though, Jim revealed to me that his Gypsy father had joined the navy and that Jim had spent many of his formative years living in the naval family quarters, or on a small farm the family had owned. Despite his open antagonism to school, he had attended school himself. In his adolescence he had joined other family members in a more traditional travelling lifestyle. Jim therefore knew both worlds and in the eyes of some on the site might also not be considered a 'real Gypsy'. Despite the conservatism of Gypsies such as Jim Hadley and the cultural rigidity and distancing they advocated, such a stance was not always feasible or supported by the actual lives of those who urged others to conform to their ideals.

Whether or not it was countenanced by the community, change was inevitable. The new and different circumstances in which the younger generation found themselves, compared with the older generation, were bound to provoke profound change. We saw in Chapter 3 that there was a growing number of one-parent (female-headed) families at South Forest, and that this had consequences for traditional family socialization practices: it was harder for the boys to go and work with their fathers, and this could lead to inactivity and depression among male non-attenders at school. Dependency on welfare was increasing due to health issues such as depression and restrictions on employment.

Many of the changes I have described had been imposed and were clearly negative. Of most concern was the dangerous vacuum that some of the younger Gypsies appeared to be in. They were benefiting neither from formal education nor the socialization practices of their family, leaving them unskilled and susceptible to low self-esteem. A question, then, was whether the strategies the resisters were adopting were sustainable. There was a danger that their distancing strategies could create a cultural enclave, leading to the Gypsy community of South Forest rejecting tools such as formal education that could assist them in increasing their inclusion. Moreover, hostility to outsiders, especially new arrivals, carried the risk of them failing to identify the primary actors responsible for their marginalization. Instead, in a process of dual closure, other vulnerable groups were blamed and the maintenance of symbolic capital led to protracted disputes, not only with these groups but with institutions such as school – disputes that reinforced negative and damaging stereotypes of Gypsies and Travellers. A form of cultural conservatism, based upon notions of ideal behaviour that did not match the reality of life for the advocates of this code, did not facilitate the process of adaptation or the creation of alternative responses to exclusion.

Some Gypsies embraced change, however. For many of the mainstreamers, the challenges of living in housing or working in the waged economy led to the development of new coping strategies that included greater participation in formal schooling. However, it is debatable how effective these new strategies were, as many of the mainstreamers found they had narrower social networks on the estate than in the past, many were employed in low-waged occupations and only a small number of students in this group enjoyed genuine academic success. The Gypsies on the South Forest Site in turn resented those who had moved into housing, believing they had turned their backs on their culture. The cultural conservatism of the resisters thus created a wedge between themselves and the mainstreamers, a divide that threatened to undermine a more general sense of unity and collectivity within this ethnic group.

A strong sense of being unjustly treated by wider society was a common theme in the perceptions and narratives of the Gypsies and Travellers on the site. A sense of victimization can be an important component in maintaining identity but can also create a dangerous victim culture (Woodward, 2002). The dangers of victim culture are revealed in this quotation from the Black novelist James Baldwin:

> I refuse absolutely to speak from the point of view of the victim. The victim can have no point of view for precisely so long as he thinks of himself as a victim. The testimony of the victim corroborates simply the reality of the chains that bind him, confirms and as it were consoles the jailer.
>
> (Baldwin, 1985: 78)

However, in the minds of the resisters they were not passively enduring their marginalization, but through the maintenance of their honour code were actively resisting. Youdell (2004) notes the ways in which Black students' cultural identities play a significant role in the maintenance of their self-esteem or even sense of self. A similar process may have been at work with the Gypsy students; thus, symbolic capital provided a coping mechanism that could diminish low self-esteem and fatalism, classic consequences for those who are unable to withstand the pressure of long-term exclusion. Culture for the Gypsies in my study, as for other groups, was a meaningful attempt to resist the dominant hegemonic culture through the development of a 'common culture', a place of resistance where the dominant culture cannot reach (Willis *et al.*, 1990), thus demonstrating that although individuals are born into structures not of their own making they are able to create their own meaningful action (Willis, 1977).

Rigid adherence to the 'Gypsy way' appeared to offer comfort to the Gypsies of South Forest in the world in which they now found themselves, which in many respects bore little resemblance to previous ways of life. Identity has offered a number of minorities, particularly those suffering from marginalization and profound change, an anchor and a sense of certainty in a world in a state of flux produced by de-industrialization, globalization, mass communication and conflict (Woodward, 2000). These identities can be condensed into rigid and uniform 'sameness' where 'difference' is despised. They can also manifest themselves in bitter and protracted disputes with other groups.

These processes become more oppositional, and collective consciousness and internal solidarity more intense, when change is imposed from outside (O'Connell, 1996). The maintenance of group identity often requires some form of periodic display of identity to maintain and intensify bonds between members (Royce, 1982). Within the Gypsies' cultural armoury practices such as attending fairs and occupying caravans provided this function, yet incidents of conflict between the group and 'others' such as school and the Somalis, in which symbolic capital was maintained and upheld, also served this purpose. Conflict affirmed who they were and was a means to assert their defiance towards marginalization.

No culture is static. Culture and identity are subject to continual change, evolving and in extreme cases fundamentally redefining borders and relations with others (Anthias *et al.*, 1992). As with the South Forest Traveller Site, the older generation may resist such change and denounce those who embrace it as having left the group. Change and adaptation could have been better managed and accommodated to Gypsy customs and practices if, rather than being imposed, change had been negotiated by decision-makers. In the post-war period, restrictions on nomadism, combined with a shortage of sites, forced many Gypsies and Travellers into housing (see Chapter 2). The experience of secondary schooling with its inflexible, monocultural curriculum and perceived discriminatory attitudes and practices were a further imposition.

Targeted responses from policymakers, aimed at creating living environments, educational experiences and employment opportunities, or at helping to develop existing business practices that reflected Gypsies' aspirations, could have eased the pressure of their marginalization. Such inclusive options and opportunities would have been more readily embraced and would also have created an alternative both to strategies of cultural distancing and isolation and to inclusion into the mainstream that held the danger of assimilation and cultural erosion. Inclusive policies would allow Gypsies and Travellers to attain 'accommodation without assimilation', a strategy that allows students to excel in school without losing self-concept and to participate in two cultural frames for different purposes without losing identity or loyalty to community (Ogbu, 1997).

Instead, policymakers ignored the views and aspirations of Gypsies and Travellers. Change was ruthlessly imposed, and the pride of Gypsy symbolic capital was combined with a strategy of resistance. If this is to change, policymakers need to become more responsive to the views and aspirations of this community and, in partnership with them, develop as a matter of urgency the policies that are now required to alleviate their marginalization. These comments apply not only to the members of the South Forest Traveller community but also to Gypsies and Travellers elsewhere. It would be wrong to assert that Gypsies' and Travellers' marginalization was solely the product of cultural conservatism. A failure to consider more strategic cultural adaptation was part of a problem that had been shaped by the demands and perceptions of majority society, translated into a set of policies that were assimilatory and authoritarian. This policy agenda has accentuated the marginalization that Gypsies and Travellers suffer. The state and majority society should therefore have a central role in addressing this exclusion. These themes are explored in Chapters 6 to 9.

## Reflection

To some readers it might appear that I am critical of the Gypsies and Travellers at South Forest. This is not my intention, but I feel there is a need to record not only positive manifestations of resistance but also those that could be seen as negative, so that lessons may be learnt. I stress, though, that oppressive behaviour was a by-product of marginalization and is not an inherent feature of Gypsy and Traveller culture and identity. I want to note that I grew attached to many of the families on the South Forest

Site, and their predicament drew me into wider campaigns for Gypsy and Traveller rights.

With reference to the South Forest School, I also hope that my comments are not overly critical but I feel compelled to chronicle how a failure to mediate or nurture intercultural dialogue prolonged a bitter dispute, to the detriment of the school and the Gypsies. However, as discussed, the school was beset with huge challenges, working in a deprived area with limited resources and having to deliver a national curriculum that did not always inspire students and staff.

After my observation, relations between the school and the Gypsies did improve significantly. With the support and guidance of the TES, a series of exhibitions and cultural events based on Gypsy culture involving the school and the site were staged, which prompted a greater degree of understanding and dialogue. South Forest School failed in its attempt to persuade the local authority to adopt its vision of an academy school and it was decided that the school would be phased out over a four-year period; this meant that the school would no longer accept new student intakes. Apparently, as the school contracted relations between the school management and students improved, becoming more friendly and relaxed.

After completing my fieldwork at South Forest and before the completion of my PhD, I took up a full-time post as a campaigner for Gypsy and Traveller communities, experiences that I discuss in the next chapter.

# Chapter 6

# Critical pedagogy

This chapter describes the struggle of Gypsies and Travellers to secure greater inclusion in society and their involvement in a social movement and how, through inclusive community development, those at the margins can be empowered.

The influential Brazilian theorist of community development, Paulo Freire, published his seminal work *Pedagogy of the Oppressed* in 1971 and inspired innovations in grassroots community action and mobilization, centred on critical pedagogy or 'emancipatory education'. Critical pedagogy entails dialogue and a series of questions that expose the contradictions of social and economic structures. Thus, through deliberation and reflection communities seek critical consciousness, an awareness of the localized but also structural factors that exclude them, and resolve to remedy their predicament through grassroots mobilization based on trust and mutualism. Freire notes the importance of the 'outsider catalyst' in this process, an outsider from a non-oppressed group who enters into a marginalized community acting as a catalyst for political and social change. The following case study, which explores the development of the Gypsy and Traveller Law Reform Coalition (GTLRC), reveals that an essential ingredient for success in community mobilization is deliberation and trust. The chapter also demonstrates how the process of critical pedagogy can be a tortuous one, especially where faced with the constraints of bureaucracy and the tensions caused by charismatic leadership. Outsider catalysts can be problematic as well as valuable: the intervention of such outsiders can easily lapse into colonialization.

## The Gypsy industry
The following quotations illustrate the standing and recognition that the GTLRC achieved within two years of its establishment. Ken Livingstone, Mayor of London:

> Gypsies and Travellers are one of the most marginalised groups in our society. The Gypsy and Traveller Law Reform Coalition (GTLRC) has worked hard to increase the dialogue between the Gypsy and Traveller community and those in charge of the policies and services that directly impact upon the lives of this

community. Only by consulting with Gypsies and Travellers
can decision-makers ensure that the policies and services they
develop will work to address the issues adversely affecting this
community. The GTLRC has made a valuable contribution to
this process.

(GTLRC, 2004: 2)

Kay Beard, the National Association of Gypsy Women:

When the Gypsy and Traveller people arrived here over 600 years
ago we were the first asylum seekers and although we have been in
the country for this long we have never really risen above refugee
status. Now things are changing and Gypsy and Traveller people
have a voice, the GTLRC is not only bringing people together but
making politicians more aware of the desperate need for sites.

(GTLRC, 2004: 2)

The GTLRC was formed in 2002 as an umbrella group encompassing a wide
array of Gypsy and Traveller organizations, who came together to form a
more effective lobby to persuade the New Labour Government to address
Gypsy and Traveller accommodation needs and tackle wider exclusion.

Gypsies and Travellers exist 'below the radar', a civil society term
that means that non-governmental organizations (NGOs) for a given
community are weak in terms of funding and organization (McCabe, 2010).
Ryder *et al.* (2014) note that some critics have derided more formal elements
of Gypsy, Roma and Traveller civil society as a 'Gypsy industry' in which
leaders and managers are accused of having engaged in what Freire (1971)
calls 'horizontal violence'. In other words, fellow campaigners become sub-
oppressors, by being hierarchical and disconnected from the communities
they seek to serve. In part this is a consequence of the conditions attached to
securing funding, which hold the potential to chain NGOs to weak agendas
that are service- or reform-orientated rather than radical and community-
based (Matras *et al.*, 2015; see also Vanderbeck, 2009; Powell, 2011).

Sande Lie notes with some justification:

Post-development portrays development as a monolithic
and hegemonic discourse that constructs rather than solves
the problems it purports to address. Yet post-development
itself becomes guilty of creating an analysis that loses sight of
individuals and agency, being fundamental to its development
critique.

(Sande Lie, 2008: 118)

It can also be argued that post-development theory has an inherent weakness of lapsing into an unquestioning exaltation of ethnic cultures that can promote static and narrow versions of identity.

Such critique of post-development theory can be applied to some of the analysis that is critical of Gypsy, Roma and Traveller community development; Powell (2011) reflects this defect by failing to appreciate the fluidity of identity and value of 'bricolage' and innovation. Influenced by Bauman (2001), Powell (2011) notes that emancipatory development can be individualizing and can fragment group cohesion. However, some post-development theorists argue that development can be inspired from within groups, who can review and revise community norms and tradition but also self-organize and mobilize, avoiding the pitfalls of narrow donor-driven control and manipulation (Udombana, 2000).

The trajectories leading to empowerment can be complex and can veer into other development traditions, providing a source of income, knowledge and experience but also holding the danger of subversion. Empowerment is a gradual process in which skills development is achieved in stages; the skills and expertise of outsiders has its place in this progression (Popple, 1994). In some cases, the spark for this sense of 'awareness' and inclusive community development comes from intervention by outsiders, who thus act as educators or 'catalysts for change' (Toomey, 2011). However, a careful balance must be maintained, as assistance can easily lapse into paternalism and managerialism (Cornwall, 2008). Technical and professional skills development is also an important tool for transformative empowerment (Shaw, 2008). In the mobilization of communities, only limited transformative change will come about if community organization is amateurish and under-resourced. This should not, however, preclude informal or semi-formal groupings (Williams, 2005); a mix of groups in a broad campaign and coalition, which includes well-staffed and resourced NGOs, can have transformative and emancipatory potential. This chapter provides insights into such processes.

While some detractors denounce emancipatory development, or critical community practice, as potentially eroding tradition and identity, they may be among the most effective weapons in defending and protecting the essence of Gypsy and Traveller culture and are thus in accordance with notions of inclusive community development.

## Inclusive community development

Prior to the formation of the GTLRC, the broadest grouping that had emerged in the UK was the Gypsy Council, formed in 1966 by Grattan Puxon and a number of community leaders (see Chapter 2). The Gypsy Council included Romany Gypsies and Irish Travellers, and although there were some initial tensions over joint campaigning by these communities a broad alliance remained in place. However, the Gypsy Council eventually split into several smaller organizations, which then became locked into rivalry and competition with each other, impeding the formation of a broad alliance encompassing a wide range of Gypsy and Traveller communities (Acton *et al.*, 2014). Tensions between the groups revolved around claims that it was the Irish Travellers who were responsible for antisocial behaviour and not the 'law-abiding Romanies' (Acton, 1974), or that the New Travellers were seeking to hijack traditional Gypsy and Traveller lifestyles and rights (Ansell with Torkington, 2014). Personality clashes also caused tensions and divisions, a common problem where charismatic leaders predominate, as is often the case in close-knit and bonded communities.

By 2002 the representatives of these diverse communities were willing to countenance the formation of a strategic coalition in order to prod the New Labour Government into action. The government seemed to be inert on the issue of Traveller sites, despite the growing shortage caused by the 1994 repeal of the duty on local authorities to provide sites. The shortage of sites was accentuating exclusion and community tensions (see Chapter 2). A key demand of the GTLRC was for the return of a statutory duty to provide sites.

From 2001 I had been working on doctoral research in London but had increasingly been pulled into activism (outside of the research field). I wanted to move beyond the limitations of academia and to become more directly involved in change, and I also wanted to somehow rediscover the sense of political purpose that I had had in my late teens (see Chapter 1). I was also drawn into the campaign because at the time none of the Gypsy and Traveller NGOs had a policy officer; staff tended to be focused on front-line activities. It was also evident that at that time community activists often lacked formal education and needed support to navigate the process of lobbying and policy formulation; these were roles that I gladly provided. However, such was the weight of work that my doctoral studies suffered, and when in 2003 the charity Comic Relief offered the GTLRC a large grant to employ a Policy Development Worker, I successfully applied for the post. The charity the Travellers Aid Trust was to manage the grant and formally line manage me, and a steering group of community members was to provide broad strategic direction for the campaigning.

The approach to steering the development of the GTLRC was based on inclusive community development, an inherently deliberative approach

(Darder, 2002) that gives voice and agency to those lacking formal education. In addition, it is asset-based in the sense of drawing upon tradition but is reflexive in innovating and developing those traditions (Ryder *et al.*, 2014). The GTLRC also enabled community members to acquire transformative new skill sets to build on existing knowledge and accrue the technical expertise to steer community affairs (Craig *et al.*, 2011). The role of Policy Development Worker involved building bridges and developing networks between Gypsy and Traveller communities and policymakers. Gilchrist (2009) sets out different models for community development, as shown in Table 6.1.

**Table 6.1:** Models of community development

| Model | Political framework | Typical activities |
|---|---|---|
| Consensus | Conservative Communitarian | Social planning Self-help groups Volunteering |
| Pluralist | Liberal Social-democrat | Community engagement Partnership working Lobbying Community capacity building |
| Conflict | Radical Socialist | Community organizing Campaigning Advocacy work |

Source: Gilchrist (2009: 38)

The GTLRC could be described as a hybrid of the pluralist and conflict approaches. A key focus was a pluralist approach centred on lobbying and giving Gypsies and Travellers a voice in Parliament through the creation of an All-Party Parliamentary Group for Gypsies and Travellers. This group has proven to be a highly effective forum in Parliament; it still exists and now includes Roma in the remit of its work. The group provides a forum for MPs, peers and civil servants to meet Gypsies, Roma and Travellers. Another focus of the GTLRC was capacity-building community leadership and developing a broad alliance of community voices but also service providers and policymakers across the political spectrum who wished to see measures in place to increase Gypsy and Traveller inclusion. However, the campaign was also conflict-centred in the sense that it had a strong social justice agenda that recognized intersectional oppressions. It was grassroots-based by working with Gypsy and Traveller families in localized struggles for justice, and by linking those stories and family leaders to the national campaign centred on securing legislative and policy change. This grassroots dimension of the campaign was influenced by conceptions of inclusive community development discussed earlier in this chapter, which while challenging oppressive and conservative community traditions sought to adapt and mobilize positive community traditions and traits in a quest for social justice.

As is typical of new social movements with their focus on identity and emancipation and, in turn, self-organization and self-determination (Chesters and Welsh, 2010) the organizational structure of the GTLRC was rather flat and informal. The finances and administrative functions attached to the Comic Relief grant were administered by the Travellers Aid Trust, a charity with a long-standing tradition of community capacity-building, primarily through awarding small grants. My post of Policy Development Worker was hosted on an annual basis by the three most established Gypsy and Traveller organizations – the Gypsy Council, the Irish Traveller Movement and Friends, Families and Travellers. Aside from having offices and small staff teams, these NGOs represented, or had a long tradition of working primarily with, one of the principal Gypsy and Traveller communities, namely Gypsies, Irish Travellers and New Travellers. This gave the GTLRC a sense of being represented organizationally by the different community groupings. In addition to these established national NGOs, localized support groups and traditional community leaders were also involved. Many of these community leaders lacked any formal education and their authority rested on their strength of personality in extended family networks, rather than on formalized democratic structures. Although some evoked the language of democratic organization by labelling themselves as presidents of associations (or similar terms), they were in reality traditional charismatic leaders mistrustful of formalized community organizations. It was reasoned that these diverse groups could learn from each other to develop and progress, but also blend together in a unique campaign that reached out to different community levels. It was this breadth that gave the GTLRC legitimacy in the eyes of policymakers.

At the core of the decision-making process within the GTLRC was the steering group, which managed the broad direction of the campaign. The majority of the steering group were community members but some non-community members, primarily NGO staff, also sat on the group. There were no presidents or other such posts; all members were equal and the chairing of meetings rotated. Meetings of the GTLRC were long and meandering as efforts were made to avoid restricting discussion through rigid agendas.

Steering-group members were encouraged to link their personal experiences of evictions, forced sedentarization and homelessness with the objectives of the campaign. Such a fusion of the personal and political ensures that campaigns are rooted in the experiences of communities and hold meaning and relevance for activists (Chambers and Cowan, 2003).

Freire (1971) notes that the transformative process begins in the stories people tell about their lives; coming to know our own stories is the beginning of becoming critical. Hence, personal stories are vehicles for critical consciousness and by problematizing aspects of stories we identify political connections and develop empathy and solidarity (Ledwith and Springett, 2010). This dialogic approach to decision-making helped forge trust between the GTLRC campaigners and intercultural dialogue between the different Gypsy and Traveller groups. Consequently, not only did Gypsies, Irish Travellers and New Travellers come to understand each other but connections were made across the community spectrum between those suffering the indignities of eviction on their own land or on the roadside, living on oppressive local authority sites or forced to live in housing. Trust and empathy are very important dynamics in creating broad and vibrant campaigns, and the time invested in deliberative forums by the GTLRC was constructive in helping to bond the campaign.

An important part of the decision-making process was the support given by community elders such as the Gypsy Len Smith, who would provide useful guidance to me in my role as Policy Development Worker, in the event of a decision needing to be made urgently between meetings. Beyond established activists, the GTLRC sought to connect to the grassroots of Gypsy and Traveller communities by strategically selecting families facing eviction or other challenges, working with them and weaving their predicament into the national campaign. These case studies of injustice were used to illustrate the dilemmas facing Gypsies and Travellers, providing families with platforms and guidance to convey stories about their dilemma and recruiting such localized community spokespersons into the national campaign.

Social movements contain what can be called a 'frame' that constructs meaning for participants and steers strategy and action (Vicari, 2010). Frames are critical in social movements in portraying injustice, and defining pathways to change (Zald, 1996). They encompass three core aspects: diagnostic, prognostic and motivational. The diagnostic frame of the GTLRC centred on the 'grammar of forms of life', in other words how restrictions on nomadism had encroached on what Habermas (1984–7) terms the 'lifeworld': modernity and regulation were marginalizing previously foundational cultural assumptions, as in the case of the restrictions placed on Gypsy and Traveller nomadic traditions. In terms of injustice, there was frequent reference to the 1994 repeal of the Caravan Sites Act and the resulting shortage of sites, making the case for the return of such a duty. More broadly, the GTLRC subscribed to what Sen (1993) describes as a 'capabilities approach'. Sen argues that policies should focus on what people are able to do and be, on the quality of their lives, and on removing obstacles in their lives so that they have more freedom to live the kind of lives that they value. Thus, development should be conceptualized in terms of people's capabilities to function, that is maximizing opportunities to undertake the actions and activities in which they want to engage, to live the life they desire. For Gypsies and Travellers, these opportunities (functionings) included access to secure and decent Traveller sites where traditional cultural practices could be maintained but also access to education and other services and opportunities to develop economic activities. The GTLRC was advocating within a radical social inclusion framework, akin to a redistributive and egalitarian discourse (see Chapter 2), a policy agenda that promoted equality and intervention. It was also an agenda that enabled empowerment and co-production through the proposed creation of a Gypsy and Traveller task force to guide policy development and a critical form of multiculturalism, which would move beyond liberal and tokenistic forms of multicultural policy to provide space and agency for Gypsy and Traveller lifestyles.

The motivational dimension of the campaign was centred on 'empowerment'. It was argued that the GTLRC was giving marginalized communities a voice and opportunities to be at the centre of advocacy and decision-making. A key role for me as the Policy Development Worker was to prepare platforms for the community to articulate their aspirations by organizing meetings with MPs, ministers and civil servants, arranging conferences and helping to ensure that community members were supported in making valid contributions that involved training in advocacy techniques. Activists had differing starting points and needs; some initial contributions were limited and might even be viewed as tokenistic by some outsiders. Invariably, though, as confidence grew and skill sets developed, roles grew larger; for instance, the Irish Traveller Tom Sweeney, although illiterate, grew into an accomplished speaker at large conferences, gave insightful media interviews and engaged effectively with ministers. In fact, Sweeney became a central force in the GTLRC campaign. Rather than envisaging inclusive community development as automatically placing the community on the highest rung of a symbolic ladder of participation, given the technical skills that advocacy requires and the confidence that the marginalized require to speak in what for them are new and strange forums, it is more useful to envisage scaffolding. Such scaffolding has different starting points and trajectories, reflecting individual needs, but it should ultimately lead to the highest pinnacles of empowerment (Ryder, 2014).

The GTLRC's formation and initial lobbying, and the fact that through political and media discourse the issue of Traveller sites was climbing the political agenda, led to government departments and ministers becoming more interested in engaging with Gypsy and Traveller leaders. The resulting interactions between activists and decision-makers were frequently organized by the GTLRC. This added momentum to the motivational frame as activists felt the chances for reform were growing. Another important dimension of the campaign was 'frame transformation' (Vijay and Kulkarni, 2012), where old values and beliefs are replaced with new ones; this was reflected in shifting attitudes to equality issues. The GTLRC had wide-ranging commitments to equality, with a negotiated mission statement opposing all forms of discrimination, including on the basis of gender and sexual orientation, that was somewhat at odds with the more conservative and traditional social mores found within some sections of Gypsy and Traveller society.

The development of the mission statement had been prompted by the Chair of the Gypsy Council, Charlie Smith, who was openly living with his male partner. Charlie was also a Labour councillor and commissioner for the Commission for Racial Equality (CRE, a statutory watchdog for race equality issues that was merged with other equality agencies into the single Equality and Human Rights Commission in 2007) (Ryder *et al.*, 2014). Charlie felt that the GTLRC needed to ensure that incoming members subscribed to broader equality issues and avoided forms of dual closure (discussed in Chapter 5). There was support for the mission statement from the growing band of female activists, who had challenged traditional gender roles through their leadership and activism.

In the past, some observers had concluded that it was futile to envisage Gypsies and Travellers forming a large and coherent campaign as they lacked democratic assumptions (Smith, 1975). One long-term non-Traveller activist had also once reasoned with me that the nature of the Gypsies' and Travellers' culture would impede the development of an organized movement and that to think otherwise was no more than cultural colonialism. Besides, this observer rationalized that Gypsies and Travellers had a band of supporters and experts who could fill the vacuum created by the Gypsies' and Travellers' lack of education and organizational ability. However, this view did not recognize that such support and assistance created tensions and resentments towards outsiders, because of its implications of a 'Gypsy industry' and paternalism. In the past, this resentment had caused acrimony about the involvement of non-Gypsies such as me. I believed that more Gypsies and Travellers with the education and the requisite organizational ability were needed to come forward and fill the roles that non-Travellers were performing.

A number of us within the GTLRC had the opinion that empowerment warranted debate among Gypsies and Travellers about the nature of exclusion and where the community wanted to be, and that this debate needed to cross gender and generational divides and not be steered by a small clique of traditional male charismatic leaders. To facilitate and articulate such debate new networks needed to be formed and there needed to be wider participation in decision-making forums. There was a need for new forms of leadership that were more inclusive and versed in modern campaigning, as opposed to the continuing predominance of a 'charismatic leadership'. Such ideological emancipation necessitates a better understanding of how the structures of power oppress and exclude, leading to the forging of alliances with other marginalized groups. This stance averts the negativism of dual closure towards others at the margins and instead offers the possibility of broad coalitions of the excluded that might form effective empowerment networks (Gilchrist, 2009). These were the ideals that the GTLRC sought to nurture.

## Fragmentation and horizontal violence

The GTLRC was able to make significant progress – not only were decision-makers now meeting Gypsies and Travellers but they were committed to addressing the shortage of sites through regional spatial strategies that created an obligation to assess need and meet regional targets for site creation (see Chapter 2). Significant recognition came in 2004 when the GTLRC won the Liberty Human Rights Award 'for exceptional achievement uniting communities and campaigning for human rights for Gypsies and Travellers'. The GTLRC had had to develop at phenomenal speed, responding not just to government interest but also media onslaughts by the tabloid press, which were demonizing unauthorized encampments. These attacks became more frequent from 2004, reaching a peak with the series of articles in *The Sun* newspaper entitled 'Stamp on the camps'. To add to this pressure, the Conservative Party sought to use the public furore generated by the media to make Traveller sites a campaign issue in the run-up to the 2005 General Election. This was evidenced by Michael Howard, then Conservative leader, initiating his 'I believe in fair play' campaign, which accused Gypsies and Travellers of law-breaking and taking advantage of the Human Rights Act (Ryder, 2015b).

The pressure of trying to fulfil so many obligations in terms of engaging with decision-makers and communities and responding to attacks diverted the GTLRC from other activities such as 'storytelling', and the dialogical nature of the steering group meetings diminished, leading to frustrations on the part of some community members and the feeling that their voices were not being heard. The fact that the Travellers Aid Trust was managing the administrative aspects of the grant reduced the need for the steering group to get involved in some of the more tedious and bureaucratic aspects of project management but at the same time this created confusion and disconnection, and a perception by some community members that they were not in control.

In my role as Policy Development Worker, I had been involved in creating a wide network of interests, but servicing the network and meeting its expectations had become too great a task, given the fact that the GTLRC only had one employee. Some of these difficulties originated from the tensions of trying to fuse a pluralist model of community development with one that was more radical and conflictual. It was sometimes difficult to balance the desire to create a wide spectrum of political support in Parliament with the demands of campaigners who wanted to see the GTLRC aligned to direct resistance to evictions at Traveller sites (see Chapter 7).

Added to the tension was what has been called activist 'burnout', the acute emotional exhaustion resulting from excessive activism. Common causes of burnout are the demands of meeting the expectations of large networks and the blurring of boundaries between home and work, but a mismatch of expectations of what can be given by the community worker also plays a part (Gilchrist, 2009). These factors were responsible for the exhaustion that I and a number of GTLRC activists were suffering in 2005. Tension also resulted from fears of the consequences of engaging with decision-makers, as noted by one GTLRC Traveller activist:

> They [other Travellers] think I'm 'crackers': they see me as a bit of a traitor … I hold the key, like many Travellers, to our culture: it's sensitive, it's private, it's passionate, everything you can possibly imagine, and it is a closely guarded secret to our way of evolving. A lot of Travellers see me as a threat, they think I'm telling people like the authorities and the police too much about

us, so that they can put a rubber stamp on us and change us to
what they want us to be.

This fear of authority and decision-makers was legitimate given the
history of oppression endured by Gypsies and Travellers, but there was
sometimes a danger that the community's collective traumagenic memory
could prompt unwarranted fears. On reflection, I can see that some of my
actions prompted such fears. Before entering into the GTLRC, my first point
of contact with Gypsies and Travellers in terms of activist forums was a
renewed Labour campaign for Travellers' Rights that I had helped to re-
establish. In my parliamentary work some of the most willing supporters
were Labour MPs such as Kevin McNamara and the trade unionist Rodney
Bickerstaffe. These Labour connections were also useful in dealing with a
Labour Government and in some respects helped open doors, but they also
stoked the fears of some community campaigners as to my motivations.
In some quarters extreme stories were circulating that I was an agent of
the Labour Party, parachuted into Gypsy and Traveller communities so
that Labour could influence their campaign. Furthermore, to deal with an
increasing workload, and in an attempt to bring a clearer organization to
my work, I decided to decrease my reliance on the advice of community
elders, rationalizing that I should increasingly refer to my line management
when immediate decisions were needed between steering group meetings.
This probably alienated some senior activists and heightened a feeling of
disconnection. In truth, I felt that some of the elders were interfering too
much and that this was adding pressure to my work.

On reflection, it is also evident that I transgressed from being an
enabler and facilitator (catalyst) to being a campaigner who over-identifies
with a campaign and exerts too much personal vision. In my work as the
Policy Development Worker I had to interact with key decision-makers such
as ministers and civil servants, and with agencies such as the Commission
for Racial Equality. These interactions with decision-makers often centred
on taking delegations of Gypsies and Travellers to present their case or to
negotiate. Such meetings were very important in cementing relationships
and commitment. I realize now, though, that I became overdependent on
some activists who were by this stage more accomplished and articulate
advocates, such as Charlie Smith. I had become increasingly nervous about
some of the more charismatic leaders and their propensity to speak 'off
message' and to go off on tangents, or to recount too much of their personal
stories and fail to grasp policy detail. However, by not including some

community members in such meetings I stoked tensions and distrust and undermined transparency within the coalition.

I realize also that I was becoming increasingly frustrated at the failure of some of the charismatic leaders to democratize and turn their local organizations into deliberative forums. Although it was a policy of the GTLRC for all member groups to have constitutions and formal meetings, this was a huge challenge for some of the older and more traditional leaders, who no doubt rationalized that their informal interactions with family and friends, and their acknowledged status as a community elder, gave them a legitimate form of authority. Some of the charismatic leaders may also have reasoned that NGOs with hierarchical management boards with few Gypsies and Travellers were not that inclusive either, and that even if they were to form such an entity themselves they would inevitably be marginalized by outsiders and bureaucracy.

At the time I did not realize it but I was also becoming a charismatic leader. In general I had worked as a facilitator and enabler but almost from the start of my involvement with the GTLRC I had become too involved with the issue of evictions, working with families involved in eviction and threading their stories into the wider campaign. In this work I clashed with an equally forceful character, Grattan Puxon, who sought to mobilize the families into more militant protest tactics against evictions, while I counselled for more deliberative and community-centred approaches. The struggle between Puxon and me careered out of control into a battle of wills (see Chapter 7). I failed to detect the dangers of my wilfulness in the sphere of evictions, and in the later stages of the GTLRC this trait became more apparent.

The hybrid organizational structure of the GTLRC, reflecting modern NGO practice and traditional community approaches, was breaking down. In the last six months of the GTLRC, I seemed increasingly to be ploughing ahead and leaving others behind, simply to get things done. I focused on ensuring that meetings in Parliament or conferences took place, but I became less concerned with the process of how decisions were made as I sought to steer clear of the bickering, arguments and competition that seemed to be souring the work of the GTLRC. However, I was inadvertently adding to the tensions. In November 2005, Charlie Smith died of leukaemia and the GTLRC and I lost an important guide and mentor. The future now seemed more uncertain and, to use a popular Traveller word, I was 'addled' (unclear and confused in my thinking) – a state of mind accentuated by intense pressures in my personal life, most notably the break-up of my marriage.

The steering group members had worked ceaselessly and they were also exhausted and tired. This was not a good state of affairs.

In February 2006, the GTLRC imploded. The key factors in its demise have been identified in this chapter and little insight would be gained by recounting in depth how it unravelled. The breaking point was when I was offered a three-month secondment to the Commission for Racial Equality to work on a project to improve community relations between Gypsies and Travellers and the wider community. The trustees of the Travellers Aid Trust, the charity that formally managed the GTLRC and its grant, had sanctioned my secondment but the approval of the steering group still had to be sought. Unfortunately, the CRE manager that my line manager and I were dealing with misunderstood the complex decision-making processes of the GTLRC and thought that the Travellers Aid Trust's approval was all that was required. Consequently, a notice appeared in the internal bulletin of the CRE staff newsletter. A CRE staff member told Travellers they worked with about the news and so some members of the GTLRC steering group made accusations that a decision had been made without their permission, leading to a heated online argument. For me, this was the final straw. I resolved that the best way to end the argument and try to save the GTLRC was to resign and take up the short-term consultancy with the CRE. I feared that if I stayed the divisions would only have flared up again later.

Unfortunately the bickering continued and the GTLRC fell apart, encouraged by different actors who wanted to establish their own alliances and directions. In the wake of the GTLRC new groupings and trajectories were mapped out. Many of the groups were still willing to come together at key events or for specific campaigns, and some community members took the organizational skills they had acquired within the GTLRC to attract funding and to develop their organizations further. Some of these organizations later floundered as a consequence of austerity. Others were efficient in modelling their work on modern NGO practices and have developed strong national platforms, but some critics complain they have become managerial and disconnected. As this chapter reveals, such a trap is easy to fall into but deliberation and reflexivity are an effective safeguard against horizontal violence and this has been effectively demonstrated in the work of a number of Gypsy, Roma and Traveller organizations. On the whole, Gypsy, Roma and Traveller civil society is much more established and experienced than it was 20 years ago and could still provide an invaluable partner for policymakers in introducing a radical programme of empowerment and inclusion for these communities.

I hope this chapter leaves the reader with an appreciation of the power of coalition, and of how innovative forms of empowerment have the potential for transformative change. It is evident that such activism necessitates time, patience and compromise, but most of all deliberation, in order to nurture and sustain a pedagogy of hope. The chapter also reveals the tightrope that an outsider catalyst must walk, and how that role can veer easily from facilitation to forms of horizontal violence. This is a theme discussed in more depth in the next chapter.

# Chapter 7

# Gypsies and Travellers on the front line: Organic intellectuals and strategic ties

This chapter explores Gypsy and Traveller protest and resistance on unauthorized developments – caravan sites without planning permission – and how community advocates emerged on such sites and developed alliances and competences to aid their struggles.

## The front line

A front line can be defined as a region where the conflict between two opposing forces is at its most intense. Gypsies and Travellers are confronted with a number of front lines. As was demonstrated by the South Forest case study (see Chapter 3), housed Gypsies and Travellers, or those living on a local authority Traveller site, might be confronted more overtly with the forces of assimilation, while those on unauthorized developments and encampments (respectively, sites owned by residents but without planning permission or temporary sites located in public spaces or land owned by others) are confronted with more muscular and even violent forms of control, as manifested in legal challenge and forced eviction. In the early 2000s, unauthorized developments were capturing the attention of politicians, the public and the media, reaching a peak of moral panic with the series of *Sun* newspaper articles entitled 'Stamp on the camps' and the campaign orchestrated by Michael Howard and the Conservative Party against Traveller encampments and developments (see Chapter 2).

A sense of difference is at the core of many people's culture and this perception is at its clearest when standing at the boundary of that culture; this leads to an awareness that things are done differently 'there' (across the boundary) and the sense of threat that poses for how things are done 'here' (within the group) (Jenkins, 1996). Thus, unauthorized encampments and developments, which brought Gypsies and Travellers more closely into the orbit of the majority population, represented for them the perceived contrarian and law-breaking tendencies of Gypsies and Travellers, while conversely the Gypsies and Travellers felt that the efforts by majoritarian society to thwart the development of their sites reflected a racist agenda that demonized traditional lifestyles.

This chapter focuses on the experiences of the spokespersons that emerged on unauthorized developments, a group that can be classified as organic intellectuals, whose perceptions of societal injustices spring organically from their marginalized condition (Gramsci, 1971; see Chapter 1). Often lacking formal education, these organic intellectual Gypsy and Traveller leaders were faced with huge challenges. This prompted the development of new strategies in the form of bridging social capital that countenanced new relationships with outsiders beyond the confines of family networks in order to accrue the expertise and support to win a planning battle to legalize an unauthorized development, secure planning permission and avoid eviction. In his study of poor urban communities in the USA facing eviction, Desmond (2012) describes 'disposable ties', the intense but often temporary relationships formed between those being evicted and strangers and more casual acquaintances in order to halt an eviction or find alternative accommodation. To meet pressing needs, the Gypsies and Travellers, like the groups Desmond observed, tended to form intense relationships, but I refer to these relationships as 'strategic ties' because via these relationships they often became involved in a more public and discourse-orientated strategy than the evictees described by Desmond.

In order to mobilize such ties and bolster the chances of sites being accepted, Gypsy and Traveller site leaders have had to develop new organizational skills, which often have fused traditional Traveller coping strategies with more mainstream forms of cultural capital. This unique fusion is a form of asset-based community development that builds on existing skills and cultural practices; it is community-driven but also upskilling (Gilchrist and Taylor, 2011; Craig *et al.*, 2011). However, excluded communities with lay knowledge cannot be expected from the start to grapple with the unavoidable bureaucratic tasks involved in major transformative community development. Indeed, oppressed people sometimes do not have contextual tools and need external help. Rather than assuming that the excluded can rapidly reach the pinnacle of empowerment, that is community control, we should envisage scaffolding of differing starting points and a need for external support, where hybrid approaches to skills progression and empowerment may be required (Tritter and McCallum, 2006). This chapter provides insights into these processes.

The observations are drawn from my work as the Policy Development Worker for the Gypsy and Traveller Law Reform Coalition, an umbrella group of Gypsy and Traveller organizations and activists, which lobbied for more sites (see Chapter 6). As part of my work in this post, which I held from 2002 to 2006, I supported families on unauthorized developments, threading their localized campaigns into a national lobbying strategy. In the process I lived on one site. At times these interactions were very intense: families living on unauthorized developments and facing eviction were often under great pressure and in need of support. I had some empathy with their legal problems, having been threatened as a teenager with what seemed at the time to be an insurmountable legal challenge. As described in Chapter 1, in 1985 I and 16 other campaigners were faced with a bill of £300,000, incurred by a local authority as it sought to construct a nuclear bunker but suffered serious construction delays and security costs due to the demonstrations and protests with which we were involved. I thus knew what it meant to be embroiled in a huge legal challenge.

## Unauthorized developments

Many of the families I met on the unauthorized developments, who had moved on to land they owned and submitted a retrospective planning application, had taken this course of action because they were tired of the cycle of eviction that they experienced on the roadside. These families wanted a base from which to access health and education services and to develop the family business. Some were tired of what they perceived as the oppressive management regimes of local authority sites. The development of a site was a huge project that utilized the close bonding networks of extended family groups, who would in many cases live together on the site. It was a collective venture that involved the pooling of money, resources and labour to buy the land and develop a site. Gilchrist (2009) describes such collective ventures as 'networks of necessity'; they are often crucial mechanisms for the highly marginalized, and are based on kinship and community webs that support reciprocity and collectivity.

At an early stage in my campaign work I assisted a Gypsy called Eddie Stubbs, who was living on a local authority site in the Midlands. Eddy was deeply unhappy on the site, which he referred to as the 'reservation', and drew comfort from a piece of land he owned in the countryside, which he hoped one day to be able to move on to and develop as a private site for his family. Eddy believed that such a move would provide a panacea to the exclusion he suffered but it was also a source of anxiety that reinforced perceptions of marginalization. Eddy had already submitted an application to live on the land but this had been refused by the local authority. He felt that this rejection stemmed from the fact that he was a Gypsy and that the council was simply discriminating against him. In rejecting his planning application, the council claimed that the land was on the floodplain and therefore not suitable for habitation. Eddy had photographs taken during heavy flooding, showing his land and a tourist caravan site and housing estate nearby. In the photographs, these two sites appeared to be more waterlogged than Eddy's land. For Eddy, these pictures were evidence that confirmed that the council had been unfair in its ruling. Eddy exclaimed:

> Someone can go from city into the country and buy a cottage and that's OK but someone can't buy a plot of land and put a caravan on it – they object; it's all right for the 'yuppies' though.

Eddy asked me to assist him in his further attempts to obtain planning permission. One of my interventions confirmed some of Eddy's fears. Eddy wanted to take a small step forward: two years after the failed planning application he wanted to secure permission to place a gate on his land. I contacted the planning department and made a general enquiry about such procedures, being careful not to refer to Eddy's land. I was informed that there was no need for a formal application as a letter to the planning department would suffice. I drafted a letter for Eddy, but when he delivered it to the planning department by hand they stated that a formal application would be needed and that he would have to pay £100. A friend of mine who worked in a planning department in a neighbouring authority informed me that there was no need for a formal application but that this had probably been requested because the applicant was a Gypsy and the council feared a larger development. A perception that councils would not be fair with them led the families with which I became acquainted to believe that they would stand a better chance of getting their site passed if they initiated an unauthorized development, which involved moving on to the land and installing the basics for habitation, such as electricity, sewerage and hardstanding (concrete foundations) for the caravans. This would often be done rapidly over a period of days, before the council secured an injunction to halt development. Once in residence, the families would then prepare for the ensuing legal battle.

Part of Eddy's motivation for involving me stemmed from a belief that someone from the settled community was more likely to be treated fairly by the planning authorities than him. He said:

> The problem is, Travellers are too trusting, someone says no you can't have that, you can't do that, they take it as the truth and that's why Travellers haven't got half the things they should have.

> They won't listen to a man like me but perhaps they will take note of a man like you.

Indeed, for many Gypsy and Traveller families, the ensuing legal challenges, which involved planning hearings and even High Court cases, presented a significant challenge to comprehend arguments, as in most cases families lacked formal schooling. Closed communities often prefer self-help mechanisms to seeking redress and support from outsiders (Shukra, 2011), but the Gypsy and Traveller families on the unauthorized developments were faced with huge challenges that they could not meet alone through their community-based networks of necessity. This vulnerability was compounded not only by low levels of literacy but also by a lack of confidence – what Freire (1971) termed a 'culture of silence'. The families often found that after they had initiated an unauthorized development, local residents would call public meetings or form action groups. In part such responses were prompted by lurid reporting by the local media, both raising concerns about the impact of the site on property prices and fears of antisocial behaviour and even criminality. Spurred on by these forces, local authorities were hesitant to give ground and mounted robust legal challenges.

The legal battles that families faced on the unauthorized developments were financially draining. Some families were eligible for legal aid but where they were not the legal costs were crippling, in some cases running into tens of thousands of pounds. Also, family businesses could suffer grievously as the media coverage sometimes made local communities aware of the family and their ethnicity, and the wider public would be hesitant to use their landscaping or construction services. Some were also affected by the attitude of local people in everyday interactions, which involved curt or impolite responses from staff in pubs and shops, and in some cases an unwillingness to serve. Among the most extreme but also frequent responses were cases of bullying at school, where children aped the behaviour of their parents and ostracized and taunted Gypsy and Traveller children; this was a cause of great distress to the families.

The anxiety and stress caused by these struggles, which in some cases spanned years, could be intense, with some suffering from depression and other anxiety-related illnesses. A constant fear for the families was that they would lose the battle and have to leave the land or be forcibly evicted. Of course, for some there was the possibility of being offered social housing as a consequence of their homeless status, but many had a profound fear of the impact of living in such accommodation. One judge noted that such a cultural aversion could be comparable to a member of the settled community being offered accommodation in a 'rat-infested barn' (Clarke v. Secretary of State for the Environment, Transport and the Regions, 2002). Hence, many refused offers of bricks and mortar accommodation and preferred the idea of returning to the roadside, even though this might subject them to a cycle of eviction and disruption. A significant fear of the families was the threat of a forced eviction, which involved local authorities contracting private bailiffs and forcibly clearing the site. A report by the Geneva-based NGO, Centre on Housing Rights and Evictions (COHRE), noted as part of a fact-finding mission on evictions:

> Forced evictions ... often leave the affected communities with serious trauma, including nightmares, fears or depressions. COHRE met with several Gypsy families who had undergone evictions – in all cases the children were profoundly affected, many still prone to bedwetting, nightmares and other psychological ills.
>
> (COHRE, 2004)

As a consequence of my advocacy work I was able to observe a number of forced evictions and was deeply shocked at how the actual clearance of the sites took place, with the use of heavy machinery and fires to burn debris while families, including children, were still on the site. At one eviction where I was present, a young Traveller boy climbed under a trailer, scared and frightened by the mayhem around him. Despite being alerted to the presence of the boy, the bailiffs attempted to forcibly move the trailer, running the risk of crushing him, especially if the trailer, which was old, had come off its axle. Fortunately, the intervention of the police stopped the bailiffs from proceeding and avoided the risk of the boy being seriously injured.

The eviction at Woodside in Bedfordshire in 2002 was one of the first large-scale evictions involving bailiffs clearing an unauthorized development. It was followed by Bulkington near Nuneaton in 2003 and again in 2004, Meadowlands in Essex in 2004 and Twin Oaks in Hertfordshire in 2005. From the date of the second Bulkington eviction the local authorities stopped informing Gypsy and Traveller families of the precise date of an eviction. This was because at previous evictions a number of outsider campaigners had offered resistance and sought to thwart the eviction action. (There is more about this later in the chapter.) Councils wanted to avoid such stand-offs but these unannounced evictions accentuated the trauma of such action, as they often took place as families were waking up and preparing children for school. Most of these sites ranged in size from 10 to 20 pitches, a pitch being a plot for one family, but they could be as large as about 50 pitches, as at the Dale Farm Site in Essex. The threat of eviction loomed over many other sites. Sometimes it was averted through legal reprieve, sometimes families voluntarily abandoned sites, and sometimes eviction took place after the period covered in this chapter (2002–6).

After the Meadowlands eviction, I interviewed some of the families and the following comments provide insight into the trauma and human cost of eviction:

> Since the eviction my kids have been having really bad nightmares. One of them has been waking up in the middle of the night screaming. My youngest has been wetting their bed. One of my biggest worries is getting my kids back at their schools.
>
> (Irish Traveller mother)

> It's been very hard [since the eviction]. I was well set up at Meadowlands. I had a good little business [block paving], people round there were getting to know me and there was plenty of work. I'm now on the road. I've pulled into a council car park at the moment. My business is in ruins. I can't take my equipment round with me. I have no contacts in the area I'm in. It's a full-time job finding places to pull into. My kids are devastated – they loved their school.
>
> (Irish Traveller father)

> I can't bear this life on the road – its hell for me and my family. I'm thinking of buying some land [agricultural] and having another go [retrospective planning permission]. I'm afraid, though, of it all ending up like it did with Meadowlands, but what choice do I have. It's not like you can walk into an estate agent and say you're a Traveller and want to buy a piece of land.
>
> (Irish Traveller father)

## Strategic ties

Many Gypsy and Traveller families have become accustomed to dealing with adversity and many families are able to recount tales of brutal roadside evictions in earlier times when many more families lived a nomadic lifestyle, or give accounts of back-breaking work in the fields where families worked as seasonal labourers picking fruit or digging for potatoes for long hours and pitiful wages. To have survived as a community and to have retained a strong sense of collective identity despite centuries of persecution, indicates a strong degree of resilience among such families. Intense forms of bonding social capital had been the chief resource that families had mobilized: close family and ethnic networks in which families supported each other, pooled resources and shared emotional capital in networks of necessity. These assets carried families through hard times. However, the complex challenges involved in trying to resolve disputes over unauthorized developments, involving planning and High Court hearings, meant that traditional coping mechanisms no longer sufficed. As noted earlier, families needed to draw upon the expertise of external forces such as lawyers and campaigners, but community spokespersons also needed to come forward to act as the interface between families and sites and these outsiders and present the public face of the campaign in legal hearings, the media, public meetings and campaign events. In the process, these organic intellectuals had to fuse traditional approaches with new ones and carefully navigate between tradition and the demands of winning a complex battle.

At the centre of these struggles were the legal hearings (planning cases and High Court hearings). The complexity of these cases was great and sometimes the Gypsies and Travellers felt that councils were manipulating the law and using their extensive legal muscle to deploy lead barristers and large legal teams to unfairly beat the families. Much to the distress of Gypsy and Traveller families, during the collection of evidence for planning hearings openly racist and ill-informed submissions would sometimes be made by members of the public, claiming that the authorization of a site would lead to an increase in criminality and antisocial behaviour in the area or lead to a sharp drop in house prices.

At times the families were baffled by the complexity of the legal cases. In some court cases that I attended, rather than try to follow the labyrinthine path of the legal argument, the Gypsies and Travellers would scan carefully the facial expressions of the judge and attempt to read the judge's mind to ascertain whether they would be fair. One Traveller mumbled to me in the public gallery five minutes into a hearing: 'This judge is a bastard, I can see that, he will not do us any favours'. The harsh and unsympathetic ruling delivered by the judge may have confirmed the Traveller's initial perception.

The chances of success for the families were enhanced where a site resident could liaise closely with their legal representatives and help marshal the data and information needed to present an effective case. This task tended to fall to female site residents. Women had often had more schooling than the men, and in the past had been given the task of liaising with schools and other centres of authority. The men were not accustomed to such roles and needed to focus on the family business. They were concerned that too much publicity would be adverse to their business activities, which involved negotiating on the doorstep with members of the settled community for building or landscaping jobs. The men felt that if their face was emblazoned across the local newspaper, it could mark the death knell for their business.

These female Gypsy and Traveller organic intellectuals therefore had to muster huge organizational resources and seek to master their legal cases to the best of their abilities, which involved poring over complex and at times bewildering legal documents. As a former schoolteacher who in some cases had been working with these female campaigners over several years, I noticed how the literacy levels of these women often grew rapidly. These activists' first tentative email messages clearly demonstrated their semi-literacy and educational gaps but the women's literacy, computer skills and mastery of planning law improved, so that before long they were able to compose complex prose statements. Negotiations about, and processes of, change with reference to identity are dependent on power distribution (Scuzzarello, 2015). As we have seen, on the unauthorized developments seeking to develop strategic ties, women were often better placed to be key agents in this process, often having stronger levels of literacy and bridging social capital than their male counterparts, but it was a shift that radically changed the power dynamics on sites and the boundaries between insiders and outsiders. These cultural adaptations were not always universally accepted and could be met with resistance.

I was on one site occupied by Irish Travellers where tensions had been growing over the changing family dynamics and altered situation of the extended family in the midst of a campaign to save their site. On this occasion an argument flared up because an adult son could not see the sense of having to go to a campaign meeting with his mother and talk about the family struggle. The son's reluctance was revealed when we spoke in his caravan later in the day:

> You don't tell someone who can't drive to drive a car do you? I'm 21 now and I'll make my own decisions. Mum can be the local Traveller and have her face all over the paper but I'm not going down that road because it will fuck up my business.

A desire to assert his independence, but also a cultural fear of participating in an unfamiliar process that would lead to his public 'outing' as a Traveller, with a correspondingly negative impact on his fledgling business, were in his mind good reasons to avoid this new challenge. Later, the mother provided further insights into the fears about, and restraints on, campaigning and civic engagement, leading to many being loath to embrace such a challenge:

It's because they're treated so bad, they've seen so much garbage thrown at them. They see no future in it and quite a few are nomadic tradesmen, you have to go to people's houses with a tradesman attitude, so they will trust you with the work that needs to be done. Now if you go up the drive and say that you are a Traveller they'll march you off the drive before they get a word out of their mouth. That is why Travellers don't want to be photographed and part of organizations or Parliament, because they don't want their culture threatened, because when I go from a meeting or event I've got to go back into the Traveller community and I have to be what they are. You see I'm like Jekyll and Hyde, I've got many masks, and I have to portray myself to different traditions and cultures in different ways.

These new challenges and strategic ties could take women far outside traditional roles or the roles in which families were accustomed to seeing a wife or mother; this could cause tensions. Sometimes cultural and family tensions were avoided and there were some families where husbands and wives shared these new roles equally, most notably well-regarded campaigning couples such as Cliff and Janie Codona at Woodside in Bedfordshire, Tom and Muzelly McCready in the Midlands and Joe and Bridie Jones in Kent. Such were the skill sets that women developed that some became well known for their expertise in the Gypsy and Traveller community, and gave advice and guidance to other families (Cemlyn *et al.*, 2014). In some cases, these female leaders became involved in the national campaign for Gypsy and Traveller rights spearheaded by the Gypsy and Traveller Law Reform Coalition (see Chapter 6). It was thought that bringing to the fore campaigners who had directly suffered the vagaries of eviction and who were threatened with homelessness would inject vibrancy and avoid disconnection with those the campaign sought to serve. Some became well-known and respected campaigners and community advocates, with Janie Codona and Bridie Jones being awarded MBEs for their community roles. Gypsy campaigners from authorized sites and homes who worked for families on unauthorized developments were also recognized: Siobhan Spencer and Maggie Smith Bendall were awarded an MBE and BEM, respectively. These honours have been sources of great collective pride for Gypsy and Traveller communities.

## Liberator development

My role as the Policy Development Worker within the GTLRC led me to become involved in a number of strategically chosen unauthorized development cases in which I threaded localized disputes into the national campaign, providing platforms for community members from unauthorized developments to articulate their concerns. There was a fusion of the personal and political, which was a marked feature of the GTLRC; if campaigns and organizations are not rooted in the experiences of communities, there is a danger of the political becoming moribund (Chambers and Cowan, 2003). As discussed in Chapter 6, the GTLRC fused a pluralist model of community development with one that was centred on critical and grassroots activism. I thus assisted the Gypsies and Travellers I worked with at a local level in giving evidence to parliamentary hearings, in meetings with ministers and civil servants, and giving media interviews to the BBC or quality newspapers such as the *Guardian* and *Independent*. Although nervous at first, the Gypsies and Travellers embraced these opportunities, seeing them as an important means to counter a barrage of anti-Traveller rhetoric from the tabloids and reactionary sections of the political establishment.

In this work I sought to dovetail the actions and messages of these Gypsy and Traveller organic intellectuals with the frame of the campaign; in other words, the core message that encapsulated campaign ideals and strategies. This core message was an argument that Gypsies and Travellers were the victims of irrational forms of prejudice and that the resulting shortage of sites caused not only untold harm to Gypsies and Travellers but also to the wider community through the legal cost of enforcement and increased incidence of unauthorized encampments and developments. It was argued that a mutually beneficial solution was a national strategy on Gypsy and Traveller accommodation underpinned by a statutory duty to provide sites that would override local authority recalcitrance (Ryder and Cemlyn, 2014). To bolster this message, the GTLRC began lobbying to reach political consensus and a solution through negotiation. The pluralist dimension of the campaign was balanced by a radical mission statement that recognized intersectional forms of oppression, including economic oppression, and in tandem with lobbying the GTLRC was engaged in inclusive community development by virtue of its grassroots activism, using and adapting community traditions to achieve emancipation and social justice (see Chapter 6).

As a consequence of this message, the GTLRC discouraged forms of resistance at evictions that could be deemed as counterproductive, that is protests that could lead to violence and injury and undermine the perception that the campaign sought to foster consensus. In this respect, the GTLRC and the families on some unauthorized sites became embroiled in a tug of war as to how to respond to eviction. The GTLRC argued that families should consider the importance of the wider campaign, and the safety of their family members, and avoid a forced eviction, and that any protests should be strictly based on non-violent direct action.

Other campaigners had a different vision of how to respond to forced eviction. Grattan Puxon was not from the Gypsy community. He was educated at the elite Westminster public school and left the UK for Ireland in the early 1960s to avoid conscription and participation in a conflict in Cyprus that he did not support. Due to poverty, in Ireland Puxon took to living in a bowtop wagon. He shared stopping places with Irish Travellers and was embraced by these communities. He became a central force in the establishment of Traveller politics in Ireland in the early 1960s and then established the Gypsy Council in the UK in 1966 (Acton and Ryder, 2015b). The campaign he helped to establish can be classified as radical community development. It was often fuelled by protests about evictions of Gypsies and Travellers, thus uniting them in common cause. The protests staged at evictions were in some respects in tune with the direct action politics of the 1960s as espoused by Alinsky (1971), which through protests and conflicts looked for opportunities to reveal the unfairness of the establishment. As a former journalist, Puxon was adept at using eviction protests, which often mobilized the support of students and other radicals, to generate media attention and highlight the need for more sites.

Puxon was a resourceful and passionate campaigner, but his radicalism was not always conducive to wider coalition building; it alienated a number of influential factions in the campaign for sites that coalesced around the Gypsy Council. As had been the case at Cherry Orchard (an unauthorized encampment outside Dublin where a major eviction was threatened in 1964/5), the protests Puxon orchestrated, although couched in the language of non-violence, could be bitter and protracted, with the risk of violence. When conflict did flare up into scuffles and fights, they were often sparked by aggressive enforcement by the authorities and in such emotionally charged encounters tempers could easily fray. Critics asserted that Puxon did not always show sufficient restraint or control in these situations. In contrast, Puxon reflected the common fear of radical community development that campaigns may be too closely aligned with the agendas of service providers (Acton *et al.*, 2014). Consequently, Puxon was apprehensive about the alliances being formed with educationalists in the state education sector, and was worried that their vision of school integration might run the risk of being assimilatory. Some Gypsy and Traveller leaders and a number of educationalists perceived Puxon to be a militant who was too domineering and divisive in the campaign. Tensions on these issues led to serious ruptures in the Gypsy Council and education movement from the early 1970s (Acton, 1974).

In 1971, Puxon relocated to Shuto Orisare, a large Roma settlement in what is now Macedonia, where he aligned himself with a growing international Romani movement. After being expelled by the communist authorities in the late 1970s, Puxon spent time in Greece and then the USA, and it was thus after a series of epic adventures that he returned to the UK in the 1990s. At first, Puxon refrained from re-entering UK Gypsy and Traveller politics but by the early 2000s he had drifted back into the fray, in part motivated by the plight of the growing UK migrant Roma population and the increasing incidence of eviction against Gypsies and Travellers. It was at the evictions in 2002 that my relationship with Puxon started to come under strain. In my early encounters with Puxon I was justifiably in awe of his achievements but I was alarmed at some of the tactics he deployed in the organization of eviction protests. In these actions Puxon mobilized the support of radical groups outside of the Gypsy and Traveller community. This was my first point of concern; I felt that in the event of an eviction all that could be gained was propaganda revealing the inhumanity of the authorities, and that the media spotlight should be focused on Gypsies and Travellers and their plight rather than outsiders, but also that they should exit the site in a way that minimized their personal trauma and risk of harm.

A second point of contention was that the protestors Puxon assembled tended to construct barricades at the entrance to Traveller sites in order to deter or impede eviction. Elaborate structures were built out of scaffolding and debris including old cars, and the barricades often resembled medieval fortresses with towers and look-out points. My concern was that the physical nature of the barricade, and the force that would be needed to remove it, would increase the chance of conflict and create media images that our opponents would exploit. Puxon asserted, with some justification, that the instigators of violence were the authorities who had developed a policy framework aimed to discourage traditional Gypsy and Traveller lifestyles, which he frequently referred to as ethnic cleansing, and that enforcement was being emphasized rather than site provision. However, as I feared, the barricades did create negative perceptions for outsiders, not helped in one case where protestors used gas canisters to construct the barricade (*Basildon Echo*, 2005). Invariably at evictions, dangerous scenes ensued as the barricades were dismantled by the bailiffs. Not only did the barricades give the bailiffs some apparent justification for a physical response but the protestors assembled, who were often young and inexperienced, were not trained and prepared for evictions and the ill-considered actions of a small minority appeared to further provoke a heavy-handed approach from the bailiffs. At one of the evictions I was involved in a running battle between the macho approach of the bailiffs and the goading behaviour of some protestors.

At the eviction in Bulkington in 2004, bailiffs had to beat a retreat because a ditch with debris that had been constructed around the site was set alight at the onset of the eviction. Furthermore, a gas canister was tossed into the flames, which meant there was a risk of an explosion. The eviction was called off on health and safety grounds, but in light of this action and other stand-offs, bailiffs ceased to give clear notice of when an eviction would happen, reducing the chance that large numbers of protestors could be mobilized. However, unclear as to when an eviction would happen and having nowhere else to go, families would linger on sites beyond the eviction notice date, hoping to have more time *in situ* and in some cases misreading signals from the authorities and wishfully interpreting what was said as meaning that an eviction was not imminent.

The tensions between Puxon and me became more acute. I was fearful that Puxon's tactics, and the eviction protests, might undermine the careful lobbying campaign of the GTLRC. For his part, Puxon was fearful that the lobbying campaign was being seduced by the Westminster establishment and was being timid in the midst of a process of ethnic cleansing. He publicly avowed the principles of non-violent direct action as practised by Gandhi in the face of belligerent and violent forms of power, yet some critics argued that physical barricades and the recruitment of less-restrained outside campaigners was creating situations that could spiral out of control.

The Gypsies and Travellers on the unauthorized developments were placed in an invidious situation: not only were they having to adopt new strategies and roles to overcome considerable threats that could deprive them of their homes but they were in the middle of a tug of war and clash of wills between myself and Puxon. Sometimes Puxon and I would be equally frustrated. One of us would visit a site and persuade residents to support a certain action, then the other would visit a day or two later and overturn that action, and the see-saw process would repeat itself. Possibly families could see the merits in both courses of action and valued the support, solace and even friendship that Puxon and I could offer.

The dangers and merits of Puxon's, and indeed my, approach are discussed in more detail in the book *No Place to Call Home: Inside the real lives of Gypsies and Travellers* (Quarmby, 2013), which provides a detailed account of the largest eviction to take place, namely the Dale Farm eviction in 2011. At this eviction, which centred on the removal of a large barricade and involved the police using tasers, many of the dynamics of previous evictions were played out, albeit on a much grander scale. However, to my mind the most powerful act of protest occurred after the eviction when the families filed out of the site in a silent and dignified march followed by outsider supporters.

The activism of Puxon and me, and our clash of wills, may have veered into 'liberator' development, which can be messianic and outsider-driven. Based on the principles of Freire (1971), the role of the liberator has successfully empowered marginalized people through education and activism, but in some instances, where the community voice has not been sufficiently heeded, has seen the world in black and white and disempowered people by polarizing groups into the 'oppressed' and 'oppressors'. In their zeal for change, liberators can discount a community's traditional coping strategies or world views as being counterproductive to more transformative aims and can try to override them. In this sense, the actions of the liberator can be colonial and manipulative (Toomey, 2011).

## Catalysts and inclusive community development

Catalysts strive to help communities build their own capacities for identifying and solving problems, emphasizing autonomous action and self-reliance. I hope that there were moments when the interaction that Puxon and I offered centred on projects and campaigns that presented opportunities to learn and adapt for Gypsies and Travellers on the unauthorized developments. However, these were opportunities that Gypsies and Travellers could select and use on their terms, and their willingness to interact with both Puxon and me demonstrates a traditional Gypsy and Traveller learning strategy of learning through participation and then taking those skills in a new direction that blends old traditions with new coping strategies. The most important contributions by external agents or catalysts should be forms of inclusive community development that give agency and opportunities for skills development to those at the margins but do not reject the power and value of tradition and are 'asset based', using tradition as a resource that can be adapted to suit present challenges but still holds the potential to sway and influence more conservative community leaders who are wedded to tradition (Ryder *et al.*, 2014).

Perhaps Puxon and I were playing mutually beneficial roles in terms of relations with decision-makers, with the 'bad cop' appearing to be more challenging and subversive and creating greater support from decision-makers for the 'good cop', who seemed to be more rational in contrast. In the localized evictions of the 1960s and 1970s, such roles would be taken up by different actors during an eviction and were instrumental in securing an extension of time to stay in a stopping place or direction to a new site, allowing the authorities to placate different parties and avoid conflict (Acton *et al.*, 2014). The lobbying campaign and its emphasis on the need for a strong policy solution may have appeared more attractive to centres of power when seen in contrast to a series of forced evictions and protests. This may have been a perception of some of the Gypsies and Travellers, in particular the men who seemed to be more supportive of Puxon's stance than the women who were more aligned to my position. Traditional learning practices within the community may provide an explanation of why some on the unauthorized developments allied themselves closely with the work of Puxon and myself, mixing and blending what we had to offer with their own world view and experiences.

Inclusive community development should be a two-way process, where the catalyst learns from the communities they support. Both Puxon and I drew upon, and were inspired in our endeavours by, the courage and strength that people such as those on the unauthorized developments demonstrated in the face of adversity, and the resilience and innovation that was displayed through forms of collectivity and alliance.

Puxon and I were both outsiders, part of the long tradition of such people who have found an affinity with Gypsy, Roma and Traveller communities (see Chapter 2). Thomas Acton once described Puxon to me as a 'force', different from normal people, a figure with vision who was an important and powerful dynamic in shaping events. To some degree I appreciate now the relevance of Acton's words: such willfulness is not the norm and through my own reflexivity I can recognize the same trait within myself. Despite our prolonged contest we were in many ways birds of a feather – the degree to which that will and determination helped or hindered the communities we worked with is open to question.

The starting point of my journey into Gypsy and Traveller activism, prior to the events described in this chapter, was my attendance at a Gypsy Council meeting in the village of Avely in Essex. At that meeting there were, in addition to Puxon, Thomas Acton, Ann Bagehot, Cliff and Janie Codona, Donald Kenrick, Josie Lee and Charlie Smith, familiar names in activist circles. The meeting was an epiphany for me; I realized that the campaign for Gypsy and Traveller rights was something special and that it had at its core a unique collection of people. I was inspired and joined the campaign. Given that Puxon was the principal founder of the Gypsy Council and the catalyst for UK and indeed European activism for Gypsy, Roma and Traveller communities, there are many, including me, who owe Puxon a great debt.

The centrality that Puxon and I enjoyed in Gypsy and Traveller advocacy was probably a reflection of the lack of education and cultural capital of Gypsies and Travellers on unauthorized encampments, which made them to some extent dependent on outsider catalysts such as us. Greater levels of education could lead to greater autonomy but – as is discussed in the next chapter – can also lead to disempowerment through tokenism and hybridity, mirroring oppressive practices of hegemony and majoritarian society.

# Chapter 8

# Academic cage fighting, position taking and awakenings within Romani studies

This chapter outlines the relationship between Gypsies, Roma and Travellers and international Roma civil society and academia, and identifies means by which these entities can become more connected and relevant to the communities they seek to study and represent. Here the book moves beyond the UK to consider continental European developments in Roma issues and provides insights into the manifestations of power in academia and among Roma elites, and the role and treatment of the marginalized within academic discourse and knowledge production.

## Reflection

After the disintegration of the Gypsy and Traveller Law Reform Coalition, I decided to revive the PhD studies that I had previously postponed – the notes and fieldwork material had lain untouched in a large trunk for four years. I had grown to hate the sight of the trunk, which was a visible reminder of failed plans and a huge investment of time. Although the research had led me to become involved in activism for Gypsy, Roma and Traveller communities, changing the direction of my life, it had failed to yield more tangible results in terms of a thesis. In 2006, resumption of the PhD was a welcome distraction from the melancholia I felt after the demise of the GTLRC. I went to Budapest to rest and reflect, and spent six months musing on the data and experiences collected from research and activism.

I returned to the UK to take up a policy post with a Traveller advocacy organization but being a more formalized NGO this work lacked the dynamism of the GTLRC, which had been more like a grassroots social movement. I resolved therefore to try to complete my doctoral research while supporting myself in my new civil society post, and eventually to transfer into the field of research, where I hoped to focus on participatory research with marginalized communities. This transition was facilitated by the success of a research grant proposal I submitted via the Irish Traveller

Movement for Big Lottery Research funding, which supported me in a study of Gypsy and Traveller economic inclusion, using narrative interviews to detect intergenerational change and acts of cultural and economic bricolage (Ryder and Greenfields, 2010). After completing that study I secured a teaching post at the Corvinus University of Budapest in 2010.

Budapest being the home of a large number of international Roma NGOs, it was a good location to establish a new career. In Budapest I met like-minded activists and researchers, and with a small band of other activist-scholars established the Roma Research and Empowerment Network (RREN), which promoted participatory research and grassroots activism by hosting seminars and conferences in community venues. A high point of RREN was 'Nothing About Us Without Us?', a seminar and conference in 2014, which provided an important deliberative event for critical and emerging activist-researchers. The papers and ideas presented were further explored in a special edition of the European *Roma Rights* journal (Bogdán *et al.*, 2015). The conference and journal provided an important platform for discussion about the role Roma should play in radical social movements and research, and included calls for decision-makers and civil society to genuinely connect with Roma communities. They also called for a more intersectional agenda embracing feminism and LGBT (lesbian, gay, bisexual and transgender) rights and radical conceptions of social justice in the campaign for Roma rights.

In my research projects and writing ventures I was also influenced by the principles of participatory research, where the co-production of knowledge between academic and non-academic communities is seen as essential to more sustainable development paths. This chimed with critical race theory by giving voice and narrative to marginalized people (Ledwith and Springett, 2010). Edited books (Richardson and Ryder, 2012; Ryder *et al.*, 2014) and funded research projects were produced in partnership with Gypsy, Roma and Traveller activists and NGOs (Ryder and Greenfields, 2010; Ryder *et al.*, 2011; Ryder and Cemlyn, 2014).

Bourdieu described a field as a structured system of social positions that is occupied by individuals or institutions. Its nature defines the situation of its occupants. Moreover, Bourdieu said that the field is an arena where struggles and contests occur over the distribution of resources (Jenkins, 2007). Positions within the social field are determined by the relationship of domination, subordination or equivalence as a consequence of the access they provide to capital. The academic world I describe can certainly be described as a social field characterized by struggles to gain or maintain control, status and power.

My entry into academia coincided with a paradigm shift in Romani studies, a period of upheaval and contestation. This chapter provides insights into my experiences of academic politics related to Romani studies during what Kuhn (1962) would call a revolutionary phase, when a crisis of confidence exists in the established paradigm where the old and new conceptual world view appear to be incommensurate. As is often the case with disputes, the struggle that ensued became characterized by leading voices on both sides of the debate as a clash of polar opposites in a series of primarily online jousts that resembled cage fighting. Such sharp factionalism crowded out more nuanced thought and discussion, and the realization of the fundamental change in knowledge production that I sought. New power elites emerged, and there remains unfinished business in efforts to hear the voices of those at the margins.

## Scientism versus critical research

Some of this friction is a result of the tensions between scientism and critical research that is to be found within many academic disciplines. Academic status and hierarchy translates into power and prestige, commodities that will influence some academics not only in their choice of interpretation of the lifeworld but also in the views they hold of their rivals. Bourdieu described how academic elites seek to sacralize the institutions and practices upon which their authority rests (Wacquant, 2013), a form of cultural reproduction that, for Bourdieu, leads to 'misrecognition', where power relations are perceived not for what they are objectively but instead in a form that depicts them as legitimate in the eyes of the beholder (Jenkins, 2007). One means by which an academic can accrue symbolic capital is to claim that their knowledge production is the most objective, informed and relevant to policymakers because it is centred within the universities and conforms to standards of academic rigour and objectivity. Such researchers are imbued with the principles of scientism. Scientism puts a high value on 'pure' science in comparison with other branches of learning or culture (Sorell, 1994). Scientism, or positivism, has been nurtured by an individualist, industrial-centric society and has commodified research, squeezing out alternative forms of knowledge (Kovach, 2005).

Scientism can impede the acquisition of insights into the lifeworld of minorities. With reference to Indigenous communities ('Indigenous' is the preferred term when referring to First Nations, Métis, Inuit, American Indian and Alaska Native peoples, or other groups who self-identify as Indigenous), scientism can constrain descriptions and obscure the hybrid and heterogeneous nature of local knowledge and modes of understanding (Carothers *et al.*,

2014). Code (1991) argues that science-based epistemologies are inherently anti-feminist. Indeed, critics contend that such positivist thinking is deeply conservative, adopting quasi-scientific methods and conceptions of detachment, and that the pursuit of objective truth is delusional (Mies, 1983).

Feminist and critical researchers believe that research should be situated (standpoint theory) in the concerns of marginalized people (Harding, 1991), and that this can best be achieved through emancipatory research practices such as participatory action research (Maguire, 1987). Critical researchers argue that through scientism academics end up prioritizing research about powerless people (by powerful people) rather than research by and with powerless people on the workings and manifestations of power. It is a line of thought that diminishes the value of knowledge that is generated outside of academia or centred on more participatory and critical approaches.

## Flashpoints and position taking within Romani studies

These competing approaches to research are apparent in the field of Romani studies. Academic interest in Romani communities has its origins in the works of writers such as Johann Rüdiger (1990, originally 1782) and Heinrich Grellmann (1787) who used linguistics to identify India as the origin of Roma communities. By the late nineteenth century the Gipsy Lore Society had been formed and through its journal a small cadre of researchers emerged focused on studying the language and folkloric traditions of Romani communities. These 'Gipsylorists' felt Gypsies were in danger of losing their ancient traditions and might even disappear through intermarriage and assimilation. Critics argued that such research was hierarchical, outsider-driven and tainted by forms of romanticism that falsely interpreted change as decline (Acton, 1974).

The first serious challenges to the Gipsy Lore tradition did not develop until the 1970s, when more activist-orientated researchers such as Acton, Hancock and Liégeois emerged, questioning the distant and amateurish scholarship of the Gipsylorists (Ryder, 2015c). However, this new cadre of scholars did not completely displace their adversaries. A new group of researchers emerged from the 1990s who were professionalized, based in universities and used what they argued to be more rigorous approaches than their precursors. These researchers, working in the scientific tradition and prominent in major research projects, professed to offer expertise in policy, offering advice to policymakers in their guise as advisers and experts. Critics complained that these 'experts' were relied upon too much by policymakers and were depriving civil society actors of a role to which they might be better suited. Critics have disparaged these researchers as 'neo-Gipsylorists', although they are more academic in their approach; as with their precursors, they are deemed to be distant and hierarchical. In turn, those dubbed neo-Gipsylorists have denounced their critics as lacking scholarly detachment and academic integrity by virtue of their partisanship (Barany, 2002).

These competing approaches had some part to play in the ruptures that occurred within the European Academic Network on Romani Studies (EANRS) and the contention surrounding the European Roma Institute (ERI). The EANRS was supported by the European Union (EU) and Council of Europe to provide a forum for academic opinion on Roma issues and to direct that expertise to guide policymakers. Unfortunately, tensions were created from its establishment in 2011 by the initial failure of the EANRS to elect any Roma to the Scientific Committee and subsequently by opposition by the Scientific Committee to the establishment of the European Roma Institute (ERI). The ERI proposal was zealously championed by the philanthropist George Soros, who used his connections in the power elite to lobby for and mobilize backing from the Council of Europe. The ERI was heralded as an opportunity to provide a platform across Europe to promote Roma arts and culture and counter anti-Gypsyism.

The ERI attracted the active support of Roma prominent in leadership positions in NGOs supported by Soros as well as from a new generation of Roma PhD holders, some of whom had transferred from civil society to academia. This faction had been prominent in their criticism of the EANRS. However, the ERI did not meet with universal acclaim; academic detractors asserted that Roma expertise should be primarily located within and not outside the academy. Critics also argued that the ERI was another instance of Soros using his wealth and influence to shape and steer Roma policy at the highest levels and that it would merely give a platform to a Roma elite rather than to communities (Matras, 2015a). Some derided it as a legacy project by Soros, which would act as a monument to his philanthropy.

Opposition to the ERI was expressed in a letter to the Council of Europe from the EANRS Scientific Committee, which resulted in a letter of protest being sent from a number of EANRS members, and indeed non-members, calling for the Scientific Committee to resign. In part, such anger was prompted by the fact that the wider membership had not been consulted about the initial letter opposing the formation of the ERI. Conversely, the Scientific Committee were perturbed by the fact that the funding for the EANRS would not be extended beyond 2015 when its existing grant came to an end, but that funding would still be directed to the ERI by the Council of Europe. Tensions around the creation of the ERI were further inflamed when the Council of Europe declared that it would cease to fund the European Roma Traveller Forum (ERTF). Established in 2005, the ERTF was funded by, and had privileged access to, the bodies of the Council of Europe that deal with matters concerning Roma and Travellers. It had a secretariat in Strasbourg within the Council of Europe's premises. During the first year, elections for national delegates were organized in 40 countries. The first Plenary Assembly was attended by 67 delegates from 33 countries. Critics reasoned that, unlike the ERI, the ERTF was formed through direct elections. However, there were counterarguments that the ERTF merely had the veneer of democracy. In truth, in a number of countries largely self-appointed Roma leaderships had wrested control of the forum, which had failed to forge an effective link with Roma communities.

At times the dispute around the ERI became heated, with insinuations that the Roma championing the ERI were trading on their connections with powerful figures such as Soros and on their ethnicity, as it was claimed that their scholarly outputs and expertise were slight. Matras, one of the chief critics, declared:

> The small circle of young activists who have been pushing forward this agenda (and who launched an aggressive campaign last year against the committee of the European Academic Network on Romani Studies when it expressed concerns about plans for ERI) are hoping to fast-track their careers by getting influential jobs on the basis of their self-declared Romani ancestry, without having to produce a track record of many years of either leadership in human rights campaigns or contributions to scholarship. They wish to benefit from the stream of European funding for Roma-projects for years to come, and they want to be able to mimic the recognised scholarly authority of eminent researchers who, thanks to the EANRS, have in the past few years made a visible appearance on the landscape of European political institutions.
>
> (Matras, 2015a)

Some of the Roma involved in the ERI retorted that academia is the 'last stronghold of colonial, paternalist approaches to Roma' (Fernandez, 2016). It was their contention that a cabal of white, middle-class and largely male academics were perturbed by the thought of being displaced.

The tensions within Romani studies reveal that academics are factional groups that can be categorized according to the differing perspectives, disciplines and approaches that they adopt. A number even operate within 'packs' with defined leaders, behaviours and outlooks, formations that lead to intellectual tussles and the 'locking of horns'. Table 8.1 illustrates the factions within Romani studies.

**Table 8.1:** The scientific universe of Romani studies: The 'usual suspects' and their dispositions, stratagems and grievances

| Key characters | Dispositions, stratagems and grievances |
| --- | --- |
| **Jane:** A retired professor and a founding figure in Romani studies, she has a strong record of activism. Jane has attracted few major research grants in recent years. | 'The problem with Josh is, he has "sold out"; he is chasing money and producing tepid research. He is in effect a "neo-Gypsylorist", researching "on" Roma communities.'<br><br>'With regard to the European Roma Institute (ERI) I am "sitting on the fence"; I am worried that power elites may end up being the most powerful voice steering the ERI.' |
| **Josh:** A mid-career researcher who has attracted significant research funding. He has produced a number of reports, has published widely in lead journals and is a sought-after international expert. | 'The mistake Jane made was to allow her research to become tainted by activism; this is why she has not attracted any serious funding in recent years and has diminishing influence in policy circles. It has to be said that Jane's work has sometimes fallen into the trap of bolstering a narrow and insular form of ethnic nationalism that imposes outsider views on this community and denies them voice and agency.'<br><br>'I am concerned that Roma experts, by virtue of their ethnicity rather than knowledge, will displace informed experts.' |
| **Mikhail:** Josh's PhD student, who has decided to focus his PhD studies on exploring Roma school participation through quantitative data. He has decided to avoid activism. | 'The best way I can help the Roma is by producing objective, clinical and neutral research and let the facts speak for themselves. How will it help my research if I devote precious and limited time to activism? The critics of my research will use that activism to deny the validity of my findings. I am not going to fall into the trap of Valeria [a Roma activist scholar] and produce "dumbed down" sociology that features in low-level publications, and that is not read or taken seriously by those with influence to make change.'<br><br>'I fear that the intellectual outputs from the ERI might be tainted by activist agendas and the project is no more than tokenism.' |

| Key characters | Dispositions, stratagems and grievances |
|---|---|
| **Valeria:** Jane's PhD student; a Roma and NGO activist who is a feminst and influenced by standpoint theory. She combines activism with research. | 'I think that Josh and Mikhail have become disconnected from Roma communities – this weakens their research as they fail to validate their findings through listening to and taking note of community views, which runs the risk of disempowering Roma communities. My idea is to bring research into Roma communities and social movements and I try to write in a way that is accessible and prefer open-access publications, thus avoiding locking away my research in elitist journals that cater primarily for the academy.' |
| | 'The ERI might give the Roma an important institutional platform across Europe to challenge xenophobia. Given the vicious and sustained attacks on Roma communities, we need to have a powerful platform where our voices can be heard. Such is the under-representation of the Roma voice at the national level that a Europe-wide platform could change perceptions.' |
| **Ionel:** An early career anthropologist who has conducted a series of studies on Roma self-help mechanisms, including money lending. | 'I find some of Valeria's viewpoints rather naive. I am a trained academic researcher and have the skills to interpret community action in a manner that is scientific and valid. Valeria has become captive to those being researched; she "sweeps under the carpet" things that show the Roma in a negative light. We need to be honest, reveal the truth and challenge internal oppressions. I also have to say that Valeria may be a Roma but her professional status and lifestyle may have made her as much of an outsider as me.' |
| | 'I oppose all forms of institutional and affirmative action and thus oppose the ERI and believe that an equal citizenship model is the solution to Roma exclusion.' |

| Key characters | Dispositions, stratagems and grievances |
| --- | --- |
| **Artur**: An associate professor, self-styled critical researcher and former high-profile activist. | 'I am on a treadmill, fighting for my academic life. I have managers watching over me and monitoring my outputs and a large teaching and administrative workload. I seem to have little or no time to critically engage with the Roma communities I worked with in the past.' |
| | 'I have no objection to the ERI and would also like to see the European Academic Network on Romani Studies continue and for the two entities to work in partnership rather than opposition but feel that the priority is to have a strong grassroots Romani movement. Should we be building up from the bottom rather than from top down?' |
| **Miguel**: A Roma and local community mediator who lives in a settlement that has attracted a great deal of research and media interest because of segregationist acts by the local authority. | 'So many researchers have been here, I sometimes feel like a bug on a pin being examined under a magnifying glass. Researchers come and go but rarely do they tell us what they said or what happened to the reports. There seems to be an academic Gypsy industry churning out reports and articles; nice work for the academics but nothing seems to change for us in the ghetto!' |
| | 'I have seen a few posts on Facebook about a possible ERI and I am open to the possibilities and work that may emerge. I would be very interested in securing grants from an ERI to fund and showcase the rap music project I run with Roma youth. Roma culture is moving in new and dynamic directions, and these young Roma have some powerful messages that need to be heard.' |

| Key characters | Dispositions, stratagems and grievances |
| --- | --- |
| **Julia**: An early stage PhD researcher considering switching the focus of her PhD away from Roma communities. | 'I feel rather perplexed by the bitter and protracted disputes between academics in Romani studies that I have witnessed in the last year. Should I ally myself with activism or adopt a more scientific approach? Or is there scope to reconcile the two? I do feel frustrated by the academic squabbling in Romani studies, and often feel nervous and hesitant to enter into debates, for fear of being "shot down" by one of the established academics or being perceived as belonging to a particular faction and paying a heavy price through negative reviews of articles or grant applications.' |
| | 'I am confused by the agendas of the different factions within Romani studies and do not know what to make of either the ERI or the EANRS.' |

Despite disputes and rivalries being part of the academic landscape, the field of Romani research is facing a critical moment. The next stage of the debate, and the actions that may result, will have profound consequences not only for the strength of Romani studies as a discipline but also for the relationships between researchers and those being researched. Is there a danger that the dispute has been mere jockeying and position taking so that one elite, which happens to be Roma, can supplant an academic and hierarchical faction that has benefited from a privileged position of proffering expert advice to power elites? Will the new guard be better than the old order? Despite the change in rhetoric and academic perspectives, will there be any substantive change leading to innovation and new directions within Romani studies?

To gain insight into potential trajectories in Romani-related scholarship it is worth exploring what were the consequences of other 'awakenings' among Indigenous or ethnic minorities in academia.

## Postcolonial and Indigenous scholarship

In recent decades there has been a growing trend within academia that has sought to give voice to marginalized groups in the research process. Some of these trends constitute postcolonial research, seeking to highlight and identify the influence and bias of white power elites in knowledge production. Likewise, critical race theory has sought to empower the voices of ethnic minorities, providing platforms for those at the margins to articulate outlooks and interpretations that too often have been neglected or derided by power elites, including powerful sections of the academy. Perhaps the precursor to these approaches can be found in feminist research, which develops non-hierarchical relations with those being researched and favours emancipatory approaches that give the researched agency but also allow the researcher to express empathy and to use knowledge to bring about transformational change.

These approaches have been interwoven with Indigenous scholarship, for instance among the First Nation Tribal groups of Canada, the Native Americans of the USA and the Aboriginal groups of Australia, which not only sought to place the testimony and narrative of these marginalized groups at the centre of knowledge production but also to challenge colonial and racist discourses that upheld oppressive behaviour. Hill (2012) notes that Indigenous peoples have been left with little choice but to engage with institutions imposed upon their lands, and can only attempt to make these institutions more attentive to their needs and aspirations. Hill refers to a maxim that insists that the master's tools can 'be used to dismantle the master's house' (Hill, 2012). However, this can run the risk of Indigenous or marginalized interests being hijacked, a point that will be explored later in this chapter with reference to Spivak and Lorde. Indigenous scholarship has been prominent in civil rights movements and in lobbying the state to acknowledge historic injustices and to right wrongs. Such struggles were played out in the academy, and over time a growing number of researchers emerged from Indigenous communities and marginalized ethnic groups. Some of these benefited from forms of affirmative action in the guise of scholarships and university departments dedicated to education centred on minority, Indigenous and aboriginal studies, elevating the study of ethnic minorities and Indigenous people to the rank of a serious academic discipline (Rigney, 2005).

Despite the increased interest in critical, feminist and Indigenous approaches to research, anti-oppressive and critical research methodologies are still at the margins of the academic world and receive little attention in most textbooks on research methods. Those at the margins have been the objects but rarely the authors of research. The discomfort that those at the margins feel about adopting traditional research processes and knowledge creation has been interpreted as the result of their personal inabilities or failings (Brown and Strega, 2005). The pressures that ethnic/Indigenous scholars face within academia is evident in the following statement: 'We Indigenous scholars have always had to justify not only our humanness and our Aboriginality, but also the fact that our intellects are "rational" and that we have a right to take our legitimate place in the academy of research' (Rigney, 2005: 4–5).

Critics of Indigenous approaches to research have argued that those influenced by such scholarship have sought to thwart development that could be beneficial to these communities by essentializing community identities and trying to preserve community identity in aspic, failing to recognize the value and indeed reality of bricolage and innovation. Other critics have derided such scholarship as being tainted by activism.

Another criticism is that affirmative action that has been a tool of assistance to Indigenous and ethnic scholarship in furthering demands for recognition and empowerment can constitute tokenism. The argument is that affirmative action allows policymakers and educational institutions to appear as if they are being proactive in challenging marginalization, when in fact the fundamental structures of discrimination remain. In Canada, Frances Widdowson and Albert Howard's book *Disrobing the Aboriginal Industry: The deception behind Indigenous cultural preservation* (2008) developed the critique of affirmative action but aroused controversy by claiming that an industry of lawyers, service providers and community leaders has emerged that has syphoned off funding that could be used to alleviate the key causes of exclusion and that has no interest in addressing the fundamental causes of exclusion. Meanwhile, it was argued, acute exclusion and forms of addiction continue to take their toll among the First Nation Tribal groups.

A critic of the book notes:

> When, however, [Widdowson and Howard] attribute these social ills mainly to the corruption, nepotism and self-serving parasitism of Native institutions, they strike out in a rather unconventional and uncertain path. When they then add that the tribulations of the First Nations peoples are harmed by the culture of professional do-gooders and paid consultants who take to the courts to defend aboriginal rights, they begin to get bogged down. Accusing legal and political advocates of Native rights of capitalizing on a kind of get-rich-and-famous scheme, while remaining indifferent to the material plight of those they purport to defend strikes many as exaggerated at best and mendaciously fanciful at worst.
>
> (Doughty, 2008)

Yaron Matras (2015b) invoked Widdowson and Howard in his critique of the ERI leadership, and in the process may have repeated the same mistake of exaggeration and causing dissension that obscures what might be some useful points of discussion about relations between power structures and scholarship and activism.

## Epistemic violence

The term 'epistemic violence' is used when privileged outsider voices speak for those at the margins without understanding or legitimacy, and consequently create stereotypes, problematize communities and deny those communities agency. It can also be applied to Roma power elites who have been happy to position themselves so as to benefit from political patronage rather than challenge structural drivers that maintain and uphold oppression. There are many instances of academic and Roma power elites having been used by decision-makers as proxy voices. There is a litany of such examples in transnational Roma politics. The International Romani Union (IRU) adopted forms of national identity such as a flag and anthem, and more recently a request for nation status within the EU (Acton and Klímová, 2001). Some interpreted such actions as stratagems to accrue personal power on the part of a Roma political elite with tenuous political legitimacy or grassroots support (Kovats, 2003). Such has been the level of political jockeying and intrigue coupled with forms of hierarchism that there are now three competing IRUs, each claiming to be the legitimate representative of Roma communities.

Although the IRU only received limited political recognition, as symbolized by its non-nation status at the United Nations, the ERTF was very much a product of decision-makers wanting to establish institutional links with Roma communities through an affirmative measure initiated by the Council of Europe. The ERTF was established in 2005 and in theory democratic elections involving Roma communities were to see a forum of elected Roma delegates established to advise the Council of Europe on Roma matters. However, complaints were made that in some cases free and fair elections were not held and it was alleged that the forum was no more than a collection of out-of-touch self-appointed Roma leaders. More serious allegations were made of mismanagement and a lack of accountability in decision-making (Nirenberg, 2009).

By 2015 the Council of Europe had become disillusioned with the ERTF and it severed its financial support and official hosting of the forum; instead it vocally supported the concept of a ERI, promoted by George Soros. Will history repeat itself? Will the ERI replicate previous failures and controversies? On one level the ERI is different from previous entities in that it has attracted a highly professional cadre of Roma leaders, many of whom have PhDs and extensive experience of managing advocacy and arts and culture projects. The emergence of these highly skilled Romani activists and scholars has been described as the 'Roma Awakening' (Acton and Ryder, 2015a).

## The Roma Awakening: A note of caution and advice

A danger to which the Roma Awakening needs to be attentive is that the vanguard of this movement may become too aligned with decision-makers through affirmative measures such as the formation of a European Roma Institute. Rather than becoming a platform to help articulate community aspirations, there is the danger of being tokenistic or merely providing a platform for a Roma activist elite. The challenge that lies ahead is whether Roma communities can be more effectively mobilized and connected to national and international spheres of advocacy, of which the ERI will no doubt form a prominent part. Across Europe, virulent forms of anti-Gypsyism continue to gain traction and provoke discrimination and hostility, often fanned by reactionary forces in the political and media establishment. Coordinated Europe-wide campaigns and an articulate narrative from an ERI could have a valuable role to play in stemming such resentments.

The leadership of the ERI must walk a cultural tightrope, and care must be taken to ensure that the institute does not seek to create a monopoly on Roma culture. As well as being a fluid phenomenon, culture, which is often rooted within communities and roles performed within those communities, is something about which communities often feel a great sense of pride and ownership. There is always the danger that when institutions are involved in cultural promotion, they may be perceived as hijacking communal culture. Such sentiments may have prompted the statement by the ETRF, which declared:

> [The ERI] should avoid the folklorization and ghettoization of Roma culture. We are of the opinion that Roma culture is and must remain the property of Roma communities, and those cultural activities should be led at grassroots level and not centralized under the auspices of an international political organization. The Council of Europe and other bodies can provide valuable support and inspiration to such activities. But we must avoid any top-down imposition of a standard culture which would risk denying the rich pluralism of genuine Roma traditions.
>
> (Albert, 2014)

Forms of essentialism have helped to give minorities a frame with which to withstand marginalization. As Spivak notes, strategic essentialism can steer and mobilize resistance (Landry and MacLean, 1996). However, care is needed to ensure that such forms of identity management do not become too controlled or policed through sanctions and insular forms of identity.

The ERI will also need to demonstrate caution in relation to the academy. With reference to the experiences of Indigenous scholarship, the leadership of the Roma Awakening needs to be attentive to the inherent dangers of marginalized ethnic groups participating in efforts to make community thought and practices coherent for the academy, as there is a danger of demeaning and displacing community knowledge (Hill, 2012). Alfred (2004) argues that 'Indigenizing' the university should be a disruptive process, aimed at promoting unsettling truths towards decolonization, including the positive aspects of what it means to be Indigenous, as well as criticisms of colonialism. These are sentiments that the Roma Awakening needs to bear in mind as its members ascend the hierarchy of the academic establishment.

It will also be important to value and promote non-Roma research through the ERI, despite the long history of misappropriation by non-Roma scholars as exemplified by the 'Gipsy Lore' tradition. Transparency, reflexivity and humility can enable insiders and outsiders to understand each other better (McGregor, 2014). For the non-Roma such a process contributes to notions of critical whiteness. White identity is imbued with notions of supremacy and is shifting and situational. Creating a more critical appreciation of white identity may be a key step in eradicating the racism embodied in some forms of that identity (see Chapter 1).

The Roma Awakening also needs to avoid the trap that some Black and other race groups have fallen into of adopting binary thinking about oppression, simplifying exclusion and placing it within a context of the oppressed and oppressor, which reflects and focuses on racial difference (Moosa-Mitha, 2005). Instead, there is a need for the recognition of more complex notions of oppression, where multiple relationships are acknowledged in which one could be the oppressed and the oppressor at the same time. Binary thinking can cause unnecessary polarization and hamper alliance-building but it also obscures an understanding not only of how race and identity can marginalize but also of how these variables interact with class, gender and sexual orientation. Hence, an intersectional approach needs to be a guiding frame in the Roma Awakening.

By adopting an intersectional approach, though, the leaders of the Roma Awakening might find themselves on a collison course with the leadership of more traditional sections of Roma communities. Sometimes communities at the margins do not want 'opening up' beyond the community or to see tradition challenged, in particular in the realm of gender relations. Conflict may also arise when findings appear to reinforce existing negative stereotypes of the community (McCabe *et al.*, 2013). The critical Roma researchers of the Roma Awakening may have difficult choices to make in this respect but should be ethical in the sense that choices and decisions should be carefully balanced on the basis of human rights, fairness and social justice. In the field of Roma studies this has been reflected in recent times by researchers who have sought to navigate the tensions of cultural conservatism and pitfalls of being misinterpreted. Such difficult, even contentious research has surfaced problems of domestic violence and hypermasculinity within some Gypsy, Roma and Traveller communities. Here the journey could be perilous, as highly marginalized communities can create comfort zones for themselves through tradition and culture, which not only can create intense bonding relations that provide solace and support in the face of exclusion, but that also can exclude outsiders and oppress gender and vulnerable groups within their communities (see Chapter 5). Therefore, the leaders of the ERI will have a major challenge in reaching out to such communities in an invitation to promote and celebrate Romani culture that also provides scope for collective reflection and re-orientation. Can this be achieved without falling into the colonialist trap of forcing people into extreme forms of acculturation and assimilation?

To believe that an ERI in the role it has been assigned, which not only promotes Roma arts and culture but also offers advice to policymakers on matters beyond arts and culture, can in itself play a central role in eradicating the dangers of European racism towards the Roma runs the risk of falling into a narrow liberal multiculturalism – a notion that contends that culture and education can prevail over racism. An intersectional world view can enable the ERI to point out to decision-makers across Europe the detrimental impact that austerity and neo-liberalism have had on Roma communities, fragmenting the social contract and pushing Roma communities to the margins but also nurturing deep forms of insecurity that breed scapegoating and xenophobia.

We may be witnessing a paradigm shift in Romani studies, where new research approaches and leaderships supplant the old. If this were to take place, or even if Roma scholarship were to receive greater recognition than hitherto, care should be taken to avoid the monopolization and indeed arrogance of the positivists who denigrated and marginalized those who held a different vision of research. Corntassel (2011) contends with reference to Indigenous people that 'indigenizing' the academy nurtures 'insurgent education', which rather than mediating between world views challenges the dominant colonial discourse. While I acknowledge the value of such a mission, care is needed to avoid an overtly combative style that might polarize and sour the ability for deliberative discourse. The Roma Awakening needs to value and celebrate academic plurality and in this sense appreciate the value of dissensus. Bourdieu (1991b) describes a working dissensus as an arena that affords critical acknowledgement of compatibilities and incompatibilities. In other words, it is a space where academics from diverging intellectual traditions can at least agree to participate in constructive dialogue. Hence, despite some of the abuse hurled at those Roma leading the ERI, restraint and dignity will need to prevail, where rather than seeking retaliation they promote dialogue and bridge-building. It is encouraging that the Roma leaders of the ERI have largely chosen to ignore the denigrating rhetoric directed at their abilities and motivation. In promoting dialogue and bridge-building, the late Romani activist Nicolae Gheorghe can be a source of inspiration.

## Conclusion: The importance of the legacy of Nicolae Gheorghe

Nicolae Gheorghe (1946–2013), a Romanian Roma human-rights activist and international functionary, was one of the towering figures to emerge within the Romani rights movement. Gheorghe could be described as having a rather Platonic view on debate, welcoming dialogue with those with greatly differing views. Alas, some of the factionalism and dogfights of present-day disputes in Romani studies stoke division rather than insight and common action (Acton and Ryder, 2015a). All of us, no matter what side of the argument we adhere to in the ongoing debates in Romani studies, must not lose sight of the civility and openness with which Gheorghe engaged with his detractors and opponents. However, there is also a need to balance this with the courage and honesty that Gheorghe also displayed, which included critique of oppressive practices within traditional Roma communities but also a deep commitment to social justice. Gheorghe himself, who had been employed at the highest levels in organizations such as the OSCE (Organization for Security and Co-operation in Europe), had in his later years come to question Roma leadership and the way in which it could become disconnected from Roma communities, in particular where civil society at the grassroots was weak and underdeveloped (Gheorghe, 2013). Gheorghe was instrumental in pioneering the work of the Romanian grassroots-orientated NGO Romani CRISS and championed the need for Roma communities to work through NGOs and community activism.

Many of those active in the present Roma Awakening were inspired and guided by Gheorghe. This will be a good omen for the future, if sight is not lost of Gheorghe's wisdom. Bearing in mind the life and example of Gheorghe, we might also want to consider the term 'affirmative sabotage', where those at the margins, like Gheorghe, attain the highest positions but seek to use that position and insider knowledge to subvert and change the system. As Spivak, who coined the term 'affirmative sabotage', noted:

> I used the term sabotage because it referred to the deliberate ruining of the master's machine from the inside. The idea is of entering the discourse that you are criticizing fully, so that you can turn it around from inside because the only way you can sabotage something is when you are working intimately with it.
>
> (Brohi, 2014)

This will be the challenge for the Roma who might attain positions of status and hierarchy in the Roma Awakening within the academy and knowledge-production apparatus.

Affirmative sabotage is, however, a strategy fraught with risk. The Black lesbian feminist writer Audre Lorde (2007) felt there was a danger of tokenism in such a stratagem and argued that narrow binary thinking precluded a more intersectional understanding of the world, which was a prerequisite to transformative change. A key point was that the use of such tools would not bring about concrete change because they worked in tandem with existing structures of power. For Lorde, the utilization of tools of patriarchy or hegemony by those who are ostensibly radicals would merely subvert transformative change. As Lorde (2007) says, 'They may allow us temporarily to beat him [the master] at his own game, but they will never enable us to bring about genuine change.' As someone who has actively supported the Roma Awakening, it is now my fear that the movement may succumb to a narrow identity politics in which elite actors of Roma heritage become involved too closely in the machinations of institutional power, under the pretext and justification of affirmative sabotage. Inevitably there is a danger of tokenism, and the structures of power rather than being dismantled may be bolstered. Lorde encourages us to reflect on the value of new tools; for me, if the Roma Awakening is to have value those tools need to be premised on intersectional alliance building but they also need to reach out to the margins and empower, give voice and act as critical catalysts. To return again to Indigenous scholarships, there have been occasions when counter-hegemonic discourse has incorporated the structures, categories and premises of hegemonic discourse (Sefa Dei, 2002). Thus, there is a danger of counter-hegemonic discourse becoming hegemonic. Could this be the fate of the Roma Awakening? The question of where next is a topic for the conclusion of this book.

*Chapter 9*
# Conclusion

## Performances and education

This book has profiled a range of life strategies adopted by Gypsy, Roma and Traveller communities shaped by the social environment and suggested that identity is a fluid and evolving phenomenon rather than being primordial and fixed. Identity is articulated through performance, a shared collection of dispositions and stratagems that ethnic groups not only enact but also adapt. (See Chapter 1 for a discussion of performance and identity.) In Chapter 1, I introduced a typology devised by Acton (1974) that summarized the life strategies adopted by Gypsies and Travellers. These included: conservatism, passing, cultural adaptation and disintegration. To some degree the typology has stood the test of time as the groups and communities profiled in this book appear to have followed the different contours of these diverging trajectories.

Many of the housed Gypsies on the South Forest Estate had distanced themselves from the residents on the Traveller site, and many had embraced the world of waged labour and the ethos of school but had either assimilated (passed) or performed their identity in the shadows, hiding their culture and identity from their neighbours and the wider community, including school. Many of the Gypsies and Travellers on the South Forest Traveller Site had, in response to exclusion and traumagenic change, which had been dramatic and disorientating, wrapped themselves in the bonds of tradition. For these cultural conservatives, school was a symbol and agent of their oppression that they resisted through non-participation. However, tensions had spiralled out of control and something like a feud had developed between the school and the residents of the site. A failure by the school management to mediate understanding and inclusive educational policies impacted negatively on the school, leading to a series of disputes and to Gypsy students and parents becoming alienated from formal learning. Given the corresponding decline of the Traveller economy on the site and its failure to provide alternatives to school, the young Gypsies had limited cultural and economic manoeuvrability. The irony of their conservatism and its failure to effectively sustain a meaningful sense of tradition was that they were susceptible to cultural disintegration and impoverishment through the collapse of the Traveller economy and demoralization.

Other Gypsies and Travellers had used identity to mobilize and galvanize their energies and resources to resist exclusion, and in the course of such action had embraced innovation and cultural adaptation. Gypsies and Travellers such as those involved in campaigns to save their family sites from eviction had embraced community members, often women, devising new roles and stratagems that moved beyond the rigid confines of tradition and countenanced strategic ties with outsiders. These roles also triggered the development of new forms of cultural capital, which included improved literacy and appreciation of education as a tool for cultural preservation but also the value of activism through organized community action. Politicized forms of strategic essentialism, namely the performance of identity politics, was most evident among the Roma profiled in the discussion of the academy who were attempting to overcome the perceived hegemony of a positivist discourse in Romani studies. These highly educated Roma vanguardists, who are now coming to the fore in what has been called a Roma Awakening, have the potential to bring about a paradigm shift in how the Roma are perceived and in the role of identity and education in emancipatory struggles. However, the book has raised the question of whether this change will reach the grassroots or whether Roma at the margins will continue to be disconnected from the decisions that frame the destiny of their communities.

These diverging groups and stratagems can be described as existing in a liminal space (see Chapter 1), being in search of a direction that might lead to resolution, namely a solution to the ills with which they and their families and communities are confronted. What might the solution be?

## Recognition, redistribution and representation

Perennial questions in Romani studies and activism are what is the cause of and solution to Gypsy, Roma and Traveller exclusion. In the past, much of the discussion on these points was framed through the lens of identity politics and the assertion that racism was the primary causal factor. However, a more nuanced and complex frame of analysis may be warranted. In the wake of the financial crisis, it is evident that Gypsy, Roma and Traveller communities across Europe have been among the greatest losers. Before the crisis, many, particularly the Roma communities of Central Eastern Europe, were consigned to worklessness or precarious economic livelihoods as transition society and the embrace of neo-liberalism failed to sustain an acceptable semblance of the social contract. This situation has been compounded by the economic crisis. Austerity and cutbacks have limited the scope and desire of the state to intervene and rectify inequality. Economic crisis has also accentuated exclusion by provoking forms of scapegoating and reactionary nationalist discourses in which vulnerable groups such as Gypsies, Roma and Travellers have been prominent targets for blame in an upsurge in xenophobia.

Thus, the marginalization, exclusion and demonization to which ethnic groups such as Gypsies, Roma and Travellers are subject, is based on racism, 'othering' and the projection of stereotypes that constitutes cultural 'misrecognition'. This, alongside the 'maldistribution' or lack of services and resources, marginalizes such groups. Fraser (1995) argues that redistribution and recognition must be united in attempts to understand and challenge social injustice. However, such a course of action may require radical approaches favouring the deconstruction and destabilization of existing identities, codes and symbolic orders that enable more intersectional interpretations of identity and exclusion to come to the fore (see the discussion in Chapter 8 on intersectionalism). In addition, in place of assimilatory or liberal multicultural policies new bolder strategies may be required that empower, intervene and correct where the markets and institutions of the state hinder and impede social justice for Gypsies, Roma and Travellers. In other words, policies shaped by redistribution and egalitarianism need to supplant third-way conceptions of inclusion or policies based on austerity and neo-liberalism (see the discussion in Chapter 2 on policy discourses). In terms of the process of mediating what social justice is and how it can be delivered, we need to consider the importance and value of representation. Fraser (2007) notes how status hierarchies map on to class differentials to prevent groups such as the Roma interacting in mainstream social arenas. In other words, economic, political and cultural structures work together to deny participation. Thus, the empowerment of Roma communities premised on inclusive community development, moving beyond forms of tokenism and inclusion only of Roma elites, needs to become apparent even at the local level and work in tandem with the changes in macro policy advocated above.

In recognizing the interrelation between economy and culture, however, Fraser (2007) notes that solutions and viable strategies may take a multitude of forms. Fraser privileges transformative action that is fundamental and structural above that which is reformist and affirmative but does acknowledge that important change can stem from the latter, which can even evolve into something that becomes transformative. Hence, purist disputes over hierarchies of resistance that can revolve around the merits of universal change over affirmative measures and the pros and cons of new social movements and identity politics in contrast to economic change may not need to be so polarizing. Change and hope can be nurtured by a multiplicity of stratagems, including simple everyday actions such as performing identity, for example declaring one's ethnicity in school ethnic monitoring forms or living a traditional Traveller lifestyle. All such actions can be counter-hegemonic; in other words, a challenge to behaviour that is considered to be orthodox and mainstream by the establishment and that raises the prospect that there are alternatives to convention. Of course, the challenge in a Freirian sense is to help actors follow the logical conclusions of these actions and link their localized predicament of exclusion and oppression to wider cultural and economic meta-narratives, leading to critical consciousness.

## Education and the quest for social justice

As has been discussed, education has been an arena of oppression for Gypsies, Roma and Travellers, but it also holds the prospect for laying the foundations for effective resistance. An educationally inclusive school has been defined by Ofsted as one where the teaching and learning, achievements, attitudes and well-being of every young person matter. Educationally inclusive schools offer new opportunities to students who may have experienced previous difficulties, taking account of students' varied life experiences and needs. Inclusive schools constantly monitor and evaluate the progress each student makes and they promote tolerance and understanding in a diverse society (Ofsted, 2000). A review of the indicators for achievement and participation for Gypsy, Roma and Traveller students, as well as the case studies in this book, suggest that educational policy concerning these groups has failed to help many achieve social and educational inclusion. A lack of resources and curricular inflexibility, together with a creeping process of selection and market reforms within the education system, has compounded exclusion (see Chapter 2).

Targeted and tailored responses from policymakers aimed at creating educational experiences that reflect Gypsy, Roma and Traveller student aspirations could provide opportunities for flexible and negotiated learning experiences and keep assimilatory tendencies at bay. Free of external restraint and pressure, Gypsies, Roma and Travellers will be free to make choices and adaptations that will enable them to retain what they consider to be the best of their culture in a way that maintains and enhances economic, cultural and social capital. Such a process will create a strong and viable form of identity that can effectively challenge discrimination. For some

Gypsies and Travellers, this ideal policy context would reflect traditional aspirations and bolster cultural practices such as self-employment, entrepreneurialism, nomadism and living in caravans. At the same time, constructive and beneficial relations with the state and wider society will facilitate intercultural dialogue and partnership, creating an environment that is conducive to new and innovative forms of adaptation. This process would witness an ever-greater number of Gypsies and Travellers accessing higher education and entering into professional occupations in a way that would enable them to retain their Gypsy and Traveller identity. If social policy moves in the opposite direction, however, the danger of assimilation may increase but also lead to conflict and resistance, as in the case of South Forest. This outcome could lead to greater levels of distancing and the formation of rigid and 'reactionary' identities.

The notion of the state regulating and intervening to create equilibrium and social justice is out of fashion and has been usurped by laissez-faire notions of the small state. Strategic guidance, equality legislation and monitoring and intervention by centres of power have an important role to play; however, in creating inclusive schools, reliance on mechanical processes of change alone cannot bring about inclusive restructuring. In tandem with state intervention and regulation, forms of social learning are required in an institutional context. In schools, this could lead to forms of collaboration involving staff, students and parents in problem identification, the development of inclusive strategies and joint work in the delivery of solutions (Ainscow, 1999). Thus, 'learning communities' are formed where school staff work collaboratively with parents and students in processes of mutual learning that lead to reform of the learning environment.

In this quest for inclusive education and collaborative relationships, in a UK context a critical setback has been the demise of the national network of Traveller Education Services (see Chapter 2), which has been decimated as a consequence of austerity. Not only has much expertise, knowledge and strategic advice been lost but schools have failed to step into the gap left by the dismantling of these services. Equally counterproductive to equality issues for groups such as Gypsies, Roma and Travellers has been the extension of the academies programme, which has undermined local authority strategic control and its potential impact on equality. However, if a will to return to previous equality frameworks materializes there can be no return to the statism of the past, which for Gypsies, Roma and Travellers often exposed them to forms of paternalism and assimilation. As noted earlier, participatory forms of engagement such as 'learning communities' in schools may offset the defects of authoritarianism in a strong strategic direction in social policy.

In the search for social justice based upon recognition, redistribution and representation, civil society could have a key role to play in terms of 'emancipatory education' and has, alongside schooling, been a central focus for discussion in this book. Critics have highlighted fears of a 'Gypsy industry', where civil society and service providers offer narrow, outsider-driven and ill-thought-out initiatives. However, a dynamic civil society can play a critical role in empowering communities, shaping policy and forming the bedrock of effective national and European advocacy campaigns by ensuring that advocacy is grounded in the needs and aspirations of communities. Despite the weaknesses of Roma and Traveller civil society we should not forget that it has also played a pivotal role in nurturing one of the brightest features of the emancipatory movement for Gypsy, Roma and Traveller communities, namely a feminist and critical wing that is increasingly recognizing the value of wider alliances with other oppositional movements based not just on identity but also economic interests and that understands the intersectional (multidimensional) nature of exclusion. Civil society can be the catalyst within communities to prompt debate and dialogue about the nature of exclusion but also devise and mobilize support for solutions. In this role, civil society could also have a central role in research and monitoring, working in unison with researchers to help include Roma communities in participatory research ventures, fostering a form of inclusive community development based on dialogic processes of inquiry.

Roma and Traveller civil society has often provided the training ground and platforms for the handful of younger progressive community activists, law-makers and artists that are now taking the political and cultural stage in the Roma Awakening. However, as has been discussed, there are fears of this elite, like the non-Roma elites they are displacing, experiencing disconnection from those at the margins and the corresponding erosion of ideals and ability to secure transformative change.

## Liminal identities, reflection and self-education

In this book I have reviewed not only the experiences of Gypsies, Roma and Travellers in highly marginalized communities, school and the world of activism and research but also my own life journey. There have been a number of 'my life with the Gypsies' books; some of these have been rather self-focused, with authors using Gypsies as a canvas to understand themselves or reflect upon wider society. Some of these works have been tinged with romanticism and stereotype, others have lacked sufficient critical self-reflection. The reader of this volume will need to decide whether I have fallen into these traps. Spivak has noted how identity and our sense of self is composed of a series of complex intersecting strands consisting of ideologies, conventions, accepted wisdom, history, prejudices and intuitions, all of which can be said to animate the subject and of which we are sometimes but not always conscious (Best, 1999). For many, it is a lifetime's work to make sense of these elements; thus the journey of self-discovery and reflection will continue.

I have tried to give an honest account of my work and motivation and how these have shifted and changed. I described how events prompted me to take paths that led to me working with Gypsies, Roma and Travellers and gave some explanation of where I stand now. At the start, I revealed how I came from what can be described as an artisan economic background, with traits of working-class and middle-class identity, the latter becoming more prominent as my family climbed what they assumed was an ascending social, economic and cultural ladder. In Chapter 2 I presented a picture of young workers cutting the lagging off copper pipes in a scrapyard. This was, in fact, a vignette describing my experiences in a summer job working in the scrapyard of one of my father's business associates. Two weeks later I started university, and I described how I experienced culture shock, being the first of my family to go to university. I coped with the disorientation of university life and the rapid movement through a series of socio-economic identities as a consequence of familial social mobility, by immersing myself in Labour and peace movement activism in the 1980s, which I thought and hoped made some sense of my life experiences, providing explanation and orientation. This intense activism was also prompted by the experiences of working in the scrapyard and working with dangerous substances, and was and is an important factor in explaining my drive and motivation in securing change, traits that some might interpret as ambition and ego.

In the 1990s I tired of activism and became disenchanted by Labour politics, and focused on a teaching career and travelling and working abroad. However, in the late 1990s I had in turn tired of what had become a self-focused life, which although comfortable and at times even stimulating ultimately left me with a sense of emptiness. Such dissatisfaction and a desire to make a greater sense of my life and give it purpose led to doctoral studies on Gypsy and Traveller communities, and consequently to a career primarily focused on activism, at least until my entry into academia in 2009.

Those classified as 'white' can be not only privileged but also entrapped and victimized by white culture. There are many shades or interpretations of 'whiteness'. I hope that through reflection I have been able to chart the impact of these differing shades but also discover a form that can foster a meaningful sense of critical consciousness (awareness and understanding). Thus, the book has been in part a process of exploration based on the concept of critical 'whiteness' (see Chapter 1), where I, as what could be considered an outsider, seek to assess my value and place within transformative activism and change for Gypsy, Roma and Traveller communities. I seek to foster a cosmopolitan vision of identity that recognizes not only the fluidity and complexity of race and identity but also the importance of other variables, such as gender and economic location in the lifeworld.

In a review of the strategies and outlooks I adopted it is evident that there were times, in particular during my early days of schoolteaching, where I was full of misunderstandings and to some degree disdain for the Gypsy and Traveller students that I taught. As a campaigner there were times when I was a facilitator and I believe successfully supported the development and progression of community activists' skills in advocacy and activism. However, there were other times when I veered into a liberator mode that was messianic and outsider driven.

I hope that others, inside and outside the Gypsy, Roma and Traveller communities, can learn from my mistakes and from whatever successes I have contributed to. I think one important message is that an educator, in a school or university or a setting of community activism, should be open to reflection and change, willing to learn from the wisdom and experiences of those who might be deemed to be lacking knowledge and expertise of any worth or value in the formal sense. I was reminded of this salutary lesson on a series of recent visits to Traveller sites.

With the passage of time and an absence from the UK of nearly a decade while I was living in Hungary, my memories of the Gypsy and Traveller sites, such as South Forest, had become faint, but in the past year as I wrote this book my thoughts returned to these sites. I decided to pay a visit to South Forest and other sites. At South Forest I returned to the point where my journey in its proper sense had begun, for it was through my relationships with the Gypsies of South Forest that my real understanding of the hardships that Gypsy and Traveller communities endure had begun. The site had contributed to an epiphany in my life, prompting me to move from the world of research to activism. On reflection, I realized that I owed the site a great debt; my ease at interacting with Gypsies and Travellers and my understanding of the dynamics of a Traveller site, which had served me well in my activism, stemmed from my experiences at South Forest.

During my recent tour of Traveller sites, the families that I met still seemed to be beset with problems and the residents were still full of apprehension about the perceived threats and dangers posed by the world beyond the gates of their site. Yet it was also possible to detect the continuance of important traditions. Large family networks still provided economic and emotional coping mechanisms for the adversities they faced. The fact that these families had stayed together and wanted to be together suggested something was working in their culture. My sense was that they had something valuable that I did not possess. This realization struck me after meeting several families with children with disabilities, who needed constant care. It was evident that the large family networks on the sites gave the children and parents the support and comfort they needed. Here I had empathy, as my own son has a severe disability, and has no siblings. A growing concern on my part is who will care for my boy when my partner and I are no longer alive. This is not a concern that the Traveller residents on many sites will have, as they can be confident that care and attention will continue to be given to their family members who have disabilities, are ill or infirm by their family networks for the course of their lives.

I felt envious of such a sense of solidarity and fraternity. However, I suspected that in the future great demands would be made on this resource as Traveller lifestyles may become ever more precarious. Fifteen years ago, I suppose my criteria for the success of a site were to find a strong leader and the children succeeding in school, I still feel such attributes are important, but what might be of even greater value is the retention of a pedagogy of hope, which for Travellers like those on South Forest was articulated in a pride in identity and desire to stay with it and provide collective support to the group. This was something I now perhaps understood better than I had in the past.

I also realized that it was a desire to achieve a sense of fraternity that from my time at university had prompted me to enter into different spheres of activism in oppositional movements and to engage with those who could be regarded as liminal or outsiders, searching for an answer and some resolution. The closest I had come to achieving some semblance of fraternity was in my work with the Gypsy and Traveller Law Reform Coalition and its fracturing had left me despondent. I had sought to replicate a form of collectivity through my activist scholarship supporting the Roma Awakening but sense there is a danger of subversion and dilution as associates who are part of the Roma Awakening enter the centre of institutions they once criticized. It is important to consider whether they can attain a form of affirmative sabotage (see Chapter 8) and create change from the inside but also, as Lorde advocates, develop new tools that challenge injustice and empower those at the margins. I feel apprehensive about the potential of the Roma Awakening in its present form; I hope I am mistaken.

I feel the Roma Awakening can only succeed if Roma organic intellectuals are given the opportunity to mobilize, remaining rooted in Romani communities but able to construct transformative agendas through the use of strategic ties. As demonstrated in Chapters 6 and 7, which described how leaders emerged on unauthorized encampments and became involved in the advocacy work of the GTLRC, organic intellectuals can indeed bridge the gap between the front line and decision-making. In the present I feel I am still on a search, searching for something that may be elusive. I am still in a liminal state.

## Where next?

In part prompted by the financial crisis that started in 2007/8, the impact of austerity and the ongoing arrogance and wrong-footedness of capitalism in the twenty-first century, I have been prompted to revert to earlier forms of socialism that I held in my youth. Living in Hungary, I have witnessed the impact of austerity, downsizing and neo-liberalism, and how the resulting trauma has been manipulated by political elites in the direction of nativism, social closure and scapegoating, with clear impacts for Roma communities.

In what is left of my productive intellectual and political life, I would like to invest energy in the development of community activism, trust and the prospects of real change. The present feels like a critical turning point. Will the right decisions and choices be made? I do not want to stand on the sidelines. Somehow I want to make a contribution, and perhaps this book can be seen as a gesture in this respect. That contribution may come in the form of a return to community activism. It may be the case that the promotion of community-orientated collaborative research is the most fulfilling and productive option. I feel tired of the sterility of strategic Roma activism and academic politics, and dispirited by their manoeuvrings. I feel a need to withdraw, to find a new environment that inspires and can provide me with a pedagogy of hope. I feel it is time to return to the 'front line'. How and what role should I assume? These questions are my current preoccupations.

In the present time of austerity, reactionary populism, most notably symbolized by Brexit and the election of Donald Trump as US president, seems to be in the ascendancy. Many people seem to be in a liminal state, unsure as to what trajectory the UK will take in its future development and identity. It is easy to fall into a mood of despair. However, experience informs me that these moods and movements have appeared before and that what ultimately repelled them was progressives working together and not losing hope. Therefore, I feel there is much still to do and all to play for, but transformative action needs to draw careful lessons from the successes and failures of previous emancipatory movements and place deliberation and inclusive community development at the centre of its work, avoiding duplicity with the manoeuvrings of power elites.

Turner (1995) notes the sense of solidarity that can exist within groups in the liminal stage, a state he described as 'communitas'. But that state is temporary and dissolves when resolution is achieved and the group reintegrates into the mass. Where reintegration is not achieved, the group forms a definable new group – a 'normative community'. A question about the groups discussed in this book is whether they will arrive at their destination (a state of existence where they wish to be). If they do, how might the structure they hope to rejoin be changed by the re-entry of a group who have been distinctly reformed? Alternatively, will the groups be mere aberrations, perpetually at the periphery?

The vanguardists, as represented by the organic intellectual Gypsies and Travellers fighting to save their family sites and the more conventionally academic intellectuals of the Roma Awakening, have indeed made great advances. These advances reveal aspects of the agendas voiced by the vanguardists, reflected in more fluid notions of gender and identity and interaction with wider society and institutions such as school, as well as changing the perceptions of some of the majority population. In contrast, forms of conservatism as reflected in bonded Roma communities have led to isolation compounded by racism, segregation and acute forms of poverty. Of course, the choices may not be so simple, but questions arise: Are the vanguardists of the Roma Awakening susceptible to forms of acculturation that induce assimilation? Are they disconnected from the margins? Of course, the vanguardists on the unauthorized sites can be said to have negotiated strategies to retain and simultaneously innovate and adapt tradition by being grounded within their communities. Both strategies relied upon the use and development of cultural capital and formal education that departed from tradition. It remains unclear as to how collective Gypsy, Roma and Traveller identity might be articulated and performed in the future. This book has given a glimpse into an ongoing phenomenon during a critical time of change.

Spivak (1988) asked the question of whether the subaltern (those at the margins) can speak for themselves. Cultural repression and marginalization limits the scope for this, as does epistemic violence. Forms of scientism and a hierarchical approach to research, discussed in Chapter 8, run the risk of producing epistemic violence by denying those at the margins voice and agency in knowledge production. In the past there may have been occasions when I have fallen into such a trap. However, I hope that I have given some voice to a community that is rarely heard by setting out in detail, and through a call to context, diverging strategies and performances devised by those at the margins of society. I hope that in this book I have presented the dangers of trying to speak for the subaltern but also presented a positive message in the sense that those at the margins can mobilize and present resistance. I have demonstrated that resistance can veer into forms of reactionary ethnicity, nativism and tokenism but there is also the possibility that through inclusive community development encompassing ethnic identity traits and traditions, culture can be adapted and re-orientated, and with the use of strategic ties alliances based on progressive and transformative agendas can be developed between group insiders and outsiders and between a heterogeneity of groups finding common cause.

I still believe in a pedagogy of hope but I am in search of new stories of resistance. I hope again to locate a counter-narrative that can inspire me and sustain me. I realize that in my life I have been lucky to have been located within, and indeed be an actor in, moments of intense performance and resistance. For instance, the campaign of the Gypsy and Traveller Law Reform Coalition, a moment when a community was under siege from a hostile media and reactionary political forces. I was also fortunate to be in a position to support and develop the early stages of the Roma Awakening and a new emancipatory Roma politics and witness and participate in the intense debates centred on Roma knowledge production and the role and function of researchers. I hope there will be other moments of being in the right place at the right time, and the joy of the warmth of fraternity and solidarity and the critical sustenance that they bring in the form of hope.

# References

Acton, T. (1974) *Gypsy Politics and Social Change: The development of ethnic ideology and pressure politics among British Gypsies from Victorian reformism to Romany nationalism*. London: Routledge and Kegan Paul.

Acton, T. (1994) 'Modernisation, moral panics and the Gypsies'. *Sociology Review*, 4 (1), 24–8.

Acton, T., Caffrey, S. and Mundy, G. (1997) 'Theorizing Gypsy law'. *American Journal of Comparative Law*, 45, 237–49.

Acton, T. and Klímová, I. (2001) 'The International Romani Union: An East European answer to West European questions?'. In Guy, W. (ed.) *Between Past and Future: The Roma of Central and Eastern Europe*. Hatfield: University of Hertfordshire Press, 157–226.

Acton, T., Mercer, P., Day, J. and Ryder, A. (2014) 'Pedagogies of Hope: The Gypsy Council and the National Gypsy Education Council'. In Ryder, A., Cemlyn, S. and Acton, T. (eds) *Hearing the Voices of Gypsy, Roma and Traveller Communities: Inclusive community development*. Bristol: Policy Press, 29–48.

Acton, T. and Ryder, A. (2015a) 'From clienthood to critique: The role of Nicolae Gheorghe as mediator and catalyst in the Roma Awakening'. In *Roma Rights 1: In search of a contemporary Roma identity: In memoriam – Nicolae Gheorghe*. Budapest: European Roma Rights Centre, 5–18.

Acton, T. and Ryder, A. (2015b) 'The Gypsy Council: Approaching 50 years of struggle'. In *Roma Rights 2: Nothing about us without us? Roma participation in policy making and knowledge production*. Budapest: European Roma Rights Centre, 11–16.

Acton, T., Acton, J., Acton, J., Cemlyn, S. and Ryder, A. (2016) 'Why we need to up our numbers game: A non-parametric approach to the methodology and politics of the demography of the Roma, Gypsy, Traveller and other ethnic populations'. *Radical Statistics*, 114, 3–23.

Adams, B., Okely, J., Morgan, D. and Smith, D. (1975) *Gypsies and Government Policy in England: A study of the travellers' way of life in relation to the policies and practices of central and local government*. London: Heinemann.

Ainscow, M. (1999) *Understanding the Development of Inclusive Schools*. London: Falmer Press.

Alasuutari, P. (1998) *An Invitation to Social Research*. London: Sage.

Albert, G. (2014) 'European Roma Institute: An answer to what question?'. *Romea*, 25 July. Online. www.romea.cz/en/news/world/european-roma-institute-an-answer-to-what-question (accessed 13 February 2017).

Alexander, J.C., Eyerman, R., Giesen, B., Smelser, N.J. and Sztompka, P. (2004) *Cultural Trauma and Collective Identity*. Berkeley: University of California Press.

Alfred, T. (2004) 'Warrier scholarship: Seeing the university as a ground of contention'. In Mihesuah, D.A. and Wilson, A.C. (eds) *Indigenizing the Academy: Transforming scholarship and empowering communities*. Lincoln: University of Nebraska Press, 88–99.

Alinsky, S. (1971) *Rules for Radicals: A practical primer for realistic radicals*. New York: Random House.

Ansell, N. and Torkington, R. (2014) 'Friends, families and Travellers: Organising to resist extreme moral panics'. In Ryder, A., Cemlyn, S. and Acton, T. (eds) *Hearing the Voices of Gypsy, Roma and Traveller Communities: Inclusive community development*. Bristol: Policy Press, 83–98.

Anthias, F., Yuval-Davis, N. and Cain, H. (1992) *Racialized Boundaries: Race, nation, gender, colour and class and the anti-racist struggle*. London: Routledge.

Askew, S. and Ross, C. (1988) *Boys Don't Cry: Boys and sexism in education*. Milton Keynes: Open University Press.

Back, L. (1996) *New Ethnicities and Urban Culture: Racisms and multiculture in young lives*. London: Routledge.

Baldwin, J. (1985) *The Evidence of Things Not Seen*. New York: Holt, Rinehart and Winston.

Ballard, R. and Ballard, C. (1977) 'The Sikhs: The development of South Asian settlements in Britain'. In Watson, J.L. (ed.) *Between Two Cultures: Migrants and minorities in Britain*. Oxford: Blackwell, 21–56.

Barany, Z. (2002) *The East European Gypsies: Regime change, marginality, and ethnopolitics*. Cambridge: Cambridge University Press.

Barth, F. (ed.) (1969) *Ethnic Groups and Boundaries: The social organization of culture difference*. Oslo: Universitetsforlaget.

*Basildon Echo* (2005) '"Gas bomb" barricade'. 2 August. Online. www.echo-news. co.uk/news/5540548._Gas_bomb__barricade/ (accessed 13 February 2017).

Bauman, Z. (2001) *The Individualized Society*. Cambridge: Polity.

Best, B. (1999) 'Postcolonialism and the deconstructive scenario: Representing Gayatri Spivak'. *Environment and Planning D: Society and Space*, 17 (4), 475–94.

Bhabha, H.K. (2004) *The Location of Culture*. New edn. Abingdon: Routledge.

Blaikie, N. (1995) *Approaches to Social Enquiry*. Cambridge: Polity Press in assocation with Blackwell.

Bogdán, M., Dunajeva, J., Junghaus, T., Kóczé, A., Rövid, M., Rostas, I., Ryder, A., Szilvási, M. and Taba, M. (eds) (2015) *Roma Rights 2: Nothing about us without us? Roma participation in policy making and knowledge production*. Budapest: European Roma Rights Centre.

Bourdieu, P. (1990) *In Other Words: Essays towards a reflexive sociology*. Trans. Adamson, M. Cambridge: Polity.

Bourdieu, P. (1991a) *Language and Symbolic Power*. Ed. Thompson, J.B. Trans. Raymond, G. and Adamson, M. Cambridge: Polity.

Bourdieu, P. (1991b) 'Epilogue: On the possibility of a field of world sociology'. In Bourdieu, P. and Coleman, J.S. (eds) *Social Theory for a Changing Society*. Oxford: Westview Press, 373–87.

Bourdieu, P. (1995) *Sociology in Question*. Trans. Nice, R. London: Sage.

Bourdieu, P. (2006) 'Structures and the habitus'. In Moore, H.L. and Sanders, T. (eds) *Anthropology in Theory: Issues in epistemology*. Malden, MA: Blackwell, 332–43.

Bourdieu, P. and Wacquant, L. (2002) *An Invitation to Reflexive Sociology*. Cambridge: Polity.

Bourne, J. (2007) *In Defence of Multiculturalism* (IRR Briefing Paper No. 2). London: Institute of Race Relations. Online. www.irr.org.uk/wp-content/uploads/2016/12/IRR_Briefing_No.2.pdf (accessed 13 February 2017).

Brod, H. and Kaufman, M. (eds) (1994) *Theorizing Masculinities* (Research on Men and Masculinities Series 5). London: Sage.

Brohi, N. (2014) 'Herald exclusive: In conversation with Gayatri Spivak'. *Dawn*, 23 December. Online. www.dawn.com/news/1152482 (accessed 13 February 2017).

Brown, L. and Strega, S. (eds) (2005) *Research as Resistance: Critical, indigenous, and anti-oppressive approaches*. Toronto: Canadian Scholars' Press.

Byrne, D. (2005) *Social Exclusion*. 2nd edn. Philadelphia: Open University Press.

Carothers, C., Moritz, M. and Zarger, R. (2014) 'Introduction: Conceptual, methodological, practical, and ethical challenges in studying and applying indigenous knowledge'. *Ecology and Society*, 19 (4), 43.

Caruth, C. (1996) *Unclaimed Experience: Trauma, narrative, and history*. Baltimore, MD: Johns Hopkins University Press.

Cemlyn, S., Smith-Bendell, M., Spencer, S. and Woodbury, S. (2014) 'Gender and community activism: The role of women in the work of the National Federation of Gypsy Liaison Groups'. In Ryder, A., Cemlyn, S. and Acton, T. (eds) *Hearing the Voices of Gypsy, Roma and Traveller Communities: Inclusive community development*. Bristol: Policy Press, 155–76.

Chambers, E.T. and Cowan, M.A. (2003) *Roots for Radicals: Organizing for power, action, and justice*. New York: Continuum.

Chesters, G. and Welsh, I. (2010) *Social Movements: The key concepts*. London: Routledge.

Code, L. (1991) *What Can She Know? Feminist theory and the construction of knowledge*. Ithaca, NY: Cornell University Press.

COHRE (Centre on Housing Rights and Evictions) (2004) Unpublished Report on UK Evictions of Gypsies and Travellers. Geneva: COHRE.

Corntassel, J. (2011) 'Indigenizing the academy: Insurgent education and the roles of indigenous intellectuals'. *Canadian Federation for the Humanities and Social Sciences Blog*, 12 January. Online. www.ideas-idees.ca/blog/indigenizing-academy-insurgent-education-and-roles-indigenous-intellectuals (accessed 13 February 2017).

Cornwall, A. (2008) 'Unpacking "participation": Models, meanings and practices'. *Community Development Journal*, 43 (3), 269–83.

Craig, G., Mayo, M., Popple, K., Shaw, M. and Taylor, M. (eds) (2011) *The Community Development Reader: History, themes and issues*. Bristol: Policy Press.

Cullen, S., Hayes, P. and Hughes, L. (2008) *Good Practice Guide: Working with housed Gypsies and Travellers*. London: Shelter.

D'Arcy, K. (2014) *Travellers and Home Education: Safe spaces and inequality*. London: IOE Press.

Darder, A. (2002) *Reinventing Paulo Freire: A pedagogy of love*. Boulder, CO: Westview Press.

DCLG (Department for Communities and Local Government) (2010) 'Time for a fair deal for the Travelling and settled community'. Press Statement by the Secretary of State for Communities and Local Government, the Rt Hon Sir Eric Pickles MP, 29 August. Online. www.gov.uk/government/news/time-for-a-fair-deal-for-the-travelling-and-settled-community (accessed 13 February 2017).

Delgado, R. and Stefancic, J. (eds) (1997) *Critical White Studies: Looking behind the mirror*. Philadelphia: Temple University Press.

Derrington, C. and Kendall, S. (2004) *Gypsy Traveller Students in Secondary Schools: Culture, identity and achievement*. Stoke-on-Trent: Trentham Books.

Desmond, M. (2012) 'Eviction and the reproduction of urban poverty'. *American Journal of Sociology*, 118 (1), 88–133.

De Vos, G.A. (1995) 'Ethnic pluralism: Conflicts and accommodation'. In Romanucci-Ross, L. and De Vos, G.A. (eds) *Ethnic Identity: Creation, conflict, and accommodation*. 3rd edn. Walnut Creek, CA: AltaMira.

DfE (Department for Education) (2016) *Revised GCSE and Equivalent Results in England: 2014 to 2015. Main national tables: SFR 01/2016 Characteristics summary table*. Online. https://www.gov.uk/government/statistics/revised-gcse-and-equivalent-results-in-england-2014-to-2015 (accessed 13 February 2017).

Department of Education and Science (1981) 'Circular 1/81 – The Education Act 1980: Admission to schools, appeals, publication of information and school attendance orders'. London: DES.

Docking, J. (1989) 'Elton's four questions: Some general considerations'. In Jones, N. (ed.) *School Management and Pupil Behaviour*. London: Falmer Press, 6–26.

Doughty, H.A. (2008) 'Review: *Disrobing the Aboriginal Industry: The deception behind indigenous cultural preservation*'. *College Quarterly*, Fall, 11 (4). Online. http://collegequarterly.ca/2008-vol11-num04-fall/reviews/doughty1.html (accessed 13 March 2017).

Douglas, M. (1966) *Purity and Danger: An analysis of concepts of pollution and taboo*. London: Routledge and Kegan Paul.

Durkheim, E. (1997) *Suicide: A study in sociology*. Trans. Spaulding, J.A. and Simpson, G. New York: Free Press.

European Commission (2014) *Roma Health Report: Health status of the Roma population: Data collection in the member states of the European Union*. Luxembourg: Publications Office of the European Union. Online. http://ec.europa.eu/health/social_determinants/docs/2014_roma_health_report_en.pdf (accessed 13 February 2017).

Eyerman, R. (2004) 'Cultural trauma: Slavery and the formation of African American identity'. In Alexander, J.C., Eyerman, R., Giesen, B., Smelser, N.J. and Sztompka, P. (eds) *Cultural Trauma and Collective Identity*. Berkeley: University of California Press, 60–111.

Farrar, M. (2012) '"Interculturalism" or "critical multiculturalism": Which discourse works best?'. In Farrar, M., Robinson, S. and Sener, O. (eds) *Workshop Proceedings: Debating multiculturalism 1*. London: Dialogue Society, 89–100.

Fernandez, C. (2016) 'Two milestones put Romani cultural discourse in the hands of Roma themselves'. *Open Society Voices,* 15 January. Online. www.opensocietyfoundations.org/voices/two-milestones-put-romani-cultural-discourse-hands-roma-themselves (accessed 13 February 2017).

Foster, P., Gomm, R. and Hammersley, M. (1996) *Constructing Educational Inequality: An assessment of research on school processes*. London: Falmer Press.

Fraser, N. (1995) 'From redistribution to recognition? Dilemmas of justice in a "post-socialist" age'. *New Left Review*, I/212, 68–93.

Fraser, N. (2007) 'Identity, exclusion, and critique: A response to four critics'. *European Journal of Political Theory*, 6 (3), 305–38.

Freire, P. (1971) *Pedagogy of the Oppressed*. New York: Herder.

Freire, P. (1994) *Pedagogy of Hope: Reliving pedagogy of the oppressed*. New York: Continuum.

Frosh, S., Phoenix, A. and Pattman, R. (2002) *Young Masculinities: Understanding boys in contemporary society*. Basingstoke: Palgrave.

Geertz, C. (1973) 'Deep play: Notes on the Balinese cockfight'. In *The Interpretation of Cultures: Selected essays*. New York: Basic Books, 412–53.

Gheorghe, N. (2013) 'Choices to be made and prices to be paid: Potential roles and consequences in Roma activism and policy-making'. In Guy, W. (ed.) *From Victimhood to Citizenship: The path of Roma integration: A debate*. Budapest: Kossuth Publishing, 41–100.

Gibson, M.A. (1988) *Accommodation without Assimilation: Sikh immigrants in an American high school*. Ithaca, NY: Cornell University Press.

Giddens, A. (1996) *In Defence of Sociology: Essays, interpretations and rejoinders*. Cambridge: Polity.

Gilchrist, A. (2009) *The Well-Connected Community: A networking approach to community development*. 2nd edn. Bristol: Policy Press.

Gilchrist, A. and Taylor, M. (2011) *The Short Guide to Community Development*. Bristol: Policy Press.

Gillborn, D. (1990) *'Race', Ethnicity and Education: Teaching and learning in multi-ethnic schools*. London: Unwin-Hyman.

Gillborn, D. (2008) *Racism and Education: Coincidence or conspiracy?* London: Routledge.

Goffman, E. (1959) *The Presentation of Self in Everyday Life*. Harmondsworth: Penguin.

Gramsci, A. (1971) *Selections from the Prison Notebooks of Antonio Gramsci*. Ed. and Trans. Hoare, Q. and Nowell Smith, G. London: Lawrence and Wishart.

Greenfields, M., Cemlyn, S. and Berlin, J. (2015a) *Bridging the Gap between Academics and Policy Makers: Gypsy, Traveller and Roma health and social work engagement*. High Wycombe: Buckinghamshire New University. Online. http://bucks.ac.uk/content/documents/Research/INSTAL/Bridging_the_Gap_Health_and_Social_Care_Report.pdf (accessed 13 February 2017).

Greenfields, M., James, Z. and Berlin, J. (2015b) *Bridging the Gap between Academics and Policy Makers: Crime and punishment: Gypsies, Travellers and Roma in the criminal justice system*. High Wycombe: Buckinghamshire New University. Online. http://bucks.ac.uk/content/documents/Research/INSTAL/Bridging_the_Gap_Criminal_Justice_Report.pdf (accessed 13 February 2017).

Grellmann, H.M.G. (1787) Dissertation on the Gipsies: Being an historical enquiry, concerning the manner of life, economy, customs and conditions of these people in Europe, and their origin. Trans. Raper, M. London: Printed for the editor by G. Bigg.

Griffin, C. (2008) *Nomads Under the Westway: Irish Travellers, Gypsies and other traders in West London*. Hatfield: University of Hertfordshire Press.

GTLRC (Gypsy and Traveller Law Reform Coalition) (2004) *Briefing*. Online. http://docplayer.net/38649450-Friends-families-and-travellers.html (accessed 13 March 2017).

Guibernau, M. and Rex, J. (1997) *The Ethnicity Reader: Nationalism, multiculturalism and migration*. Cambridge: Polity.

Haas, J. and Shaffir, W. (1982) 'Taking on the role of doctor: A dramaturgical analysis of professionalization'. *Symbolic Interaction*, 5 (2), 187–203.

Habermas, J. (1984–7) *The Theory of Communicative Action*. 2 vols. Trans. McCarthy, T. Boston: Beacon Press.

Hall, D.J. and Hall, I.M. (1996) *Practical Social Research: Project work in the community*. Basingstoke: Macmillan.

Hall, S. (1991) 'Old and new identities, old and new ethnicities'. In King, A.D. (ed.) *Culture, Globalization and the World-System: Contemporary conditions for the representation of identity*. London: Macmillan, 41–69.

Hall, S. (1992) 'New ethnicities'. In Donald, J. and Rattansi, A. (eds) *'Race', Culture and Difference*. London: Sage in association with the Open University, 252–9.

Hall, S. and Du Gay, P. (1997) *Questions of Cultural Identity*. London: Sage.

Halpern, D. (2007) *Social Capital*. Cambridge: Polity.

Harding, S. (1991) *Whose Science? Whose Knowledge? Thinking from women's lives*. Ithaca, NY: Cornell University Press.

Hare, A.P., Blumberg, H.H., Davies, M.F. and Kent, M.V. (1995) *Small Group Research: A handbook*. Norwood, NJ: Ablex Publishing.

Hargreaves, D.H. (1982) *The Challenge for the Comprehensive School: Culture, curriculum and community*. London: Routledge and Kegan Paul.

Hawes, D. (1997) *Gypsies, Travellers and the Health Service: A study in inequality*. Bristol: Policy Press.

Haywood, C. and Mac an Ghaill, M. (1996) 'Schooling masculinities'. In Mac an Ghaill, M. (ed.) *Understanding Masculinities: Social relations and cultural arenas*. Buckingham: Open University Press, 50–60.

Hemery, S. (2016) 'UK Gypsies and Travellers take a stand against discrimination'. *openDemocracy UK*, 16 April. Online. www.opendemocracy.net/uk/sophie-hemery/uk-gypsies-and-travellers-take-stand-against-discrimination-0 (accessed 13 February 2017).

Hewitt, R. (2005) *White Backlash and the Politics of Multiculturalism*. New York: Cambridge University Press.

Hill, E. (2012) 'A critique of the call to "Always Indigenize!"'. *Peninsula: A journal of relational politics*, 2 (1), 1–7.

hooks, b. (1991) *Yearning: Race, gender, and cultural politics*. London: Turnaround.

hooks, b. (1992) *Black Looks: Race and representation*. Boston, MA: South End Press.

Horvath, A., Thomassen, B. and Wydra, H. (2009) 'Introduction: Liminality and cultures of change'. *International Political Anthropology*, 2 (1), 3–4.

Ivatts, A. (2005) 'The education of Gypsy/Roma Traveller and Travelling Children'. Position Paper for the National Strategy Group. Department for Education and Skills.

Ivatts, A. and Day, J. (2014) '"Ministers like it that way": Developing education services for Gypsies and Travellers'. In Ryder, A., Cemlyn, S. and Acton, T. (eds) *Hearing the Voices of Gypsy, Roma and Traveller Communities: Inclusive community development*. Bristol: Policy Press, 49–65.

Jenkins, R. (1996) *Social Identity*. London: Routledge.

Jenkins, R. (2007) *Pierre Bourdieu*. Rev. edn. London: Routledge.

Joshua, H., Wallace, T. and Booth, H. (1983) *To Ride The Storm: The 1980 Bristol 'Riot' and the state*. London: Heinemann.

Kabachnik, P. and Ryder, A. (2013) 'Nomadism and the 2003 Anti-Social Behaviour Act: Constraining Gypsy and Traveller mobilities in Britain'. *Romani Studies*, 23 (1), 83–106.

Kendall, S. (1997) 'Sites of resistance: Places on the margin: The Traveller "homeplace"'. In Acton, T. (ed.) *Gypsy Politics and Traveller Identity*. Hatfield: University of Hertfordshire Press, 70–89.

Kenrick, D. and Bakewell, S. (1995) *On the Verge: The Gypsies of England*. Hatfield: University of Hertfordshire Press.

Keynan, H. (2000) 'Male roles and the making of the Somali tragedy'. In Breines, I., Connell, R. and Eide, I. (eds) *Male Roles, Masculinities and Violence: A culture of peace perspective* (Cultures of Peace Series). Paris: UNESCO Publishing, 189–99.

Kisby, B. (2010) 'The Big Society: Power to the people?'. *Political Quarterly*, 81 (4), 484–91.

Kovach, M. (2005) 'Emerging from the Margins: Indigenous methodologies'. In Brown, L. and Strega, S. (eds) *Research As Resistance: Critical, indigenous, and anti-oppressive approaches*. Toronto: Canadian Scholars' Press, 19–36.

Kovats, M. (2003) 'The politics of Roma identity: Between nationalism and destitution'. *openDemocracy*, 29 July. Online. www.opendemocracy.net/people-migrationeurope/article_1399.jsp (accessed 13 February 2017).

Kriesberg, L. (2003) *Constructive Conflicts: From escalation to resolution*. 2nd edn. Lanham, MD: Rowman and Littlefield.

Kuhn, T.S. (1962) *The Structure of Scientific Revolutions*. Chicago: University of Chicago Press.

Landry, D. and MacLean, G. (eds) (1996) *The Spivak Reader: Selected works of Gayatri Chakravorty Spivak*. New York: Routledge.

Ledwith, M. and Springett, J. (2010) *Participatory Practice: Community-based action for transformative change*. Bristol: Policy Press.

Levinson, M.P. and Sparkes, A.C. (2003) 'Gypsy masculinities and the school-home interface: Exploring contradictions and tensions'. *British Journal of Sociology of Education*, 24 (5), 587–603.

Levitas, R. (1998) *The Inclusive Society? Social exclusion and New Labour*. Basingstoke: Macmillan.

Liégeois, J.-P. (1998) *School Provision for Ethnic Minorities: The Gypsy paradigm*. Trans. ní Shuinéar, S. New edn. Hatfield: University of Hertfordshire Press.

Lorde, A. (2007) 'The master's tools will never dismantle the master's house'. In *Sister Outsider: Essays and speeches*. New edn. Berkeley, CA: Crossing Press, 110–14.

Maguire, P. (1987) *Doing Participatory Research: A feminist approach*. Amherst: Center for International Education, University of Massachusetts.

Majors, R. and Billson, J.M. (1992) *Cool Pose: The dilemmas of Black manhood in America*. New York: Lexington.

Majors, R., Taylor, R., Peden, B. and Hall, R.E. (1994) 'Cool Pose: A symbolic mechanism for masculine role enactment and coping by Black males'. In Majors, R.G. and Gordon, J.U. (eds) *The American Black Male: His present status and his future*. Chicago: Nelson-Hall, 245–59.

Matras, Y. (2015a) 'Commentary: Why are they setting up a European Roma Institute?'. *Romea*, 5 April. Online. www.romea.cz/en/news/world/commentary-why-are-they-setting-up-a-european-roma-institute (accessed 13 February 2017).

Matras, Y. (2015b) 'Why plans for a European Roma Institute might be a setback for Europe's Roma'. *LSE EUROPP Blog*, 16 April. Online. http://blogs.lse.ac.uk/europpblog/2015/04/16/why-plans-for-a-european-roma-institute-might-be-a-setback-for-europes-roma/ (accessed 13 February 2017).

Matras, Y., Leggio, D.V. and Steel, M. (2015) '"Roma education" as a lucrative niche: Ideologies and representations'. *Zeitschrift fuer Internationale Bildungsforschung und Entwicklungspaedagogik*, 38 (1), 11–17.

Mayall, D. (1988) *Gypsy-Travellers in Nineteenth-Century Society*. Cambridge: Cambridge University Press.

Mayall, D. (2004) *Gypsy Identities, 1500–2000: From Egipcyans and Moon-men to the ethnic Romany*. London: Routledge.

McCabe, A. (2010) *Below the Radar in a Big Society? Reflections on community engagement, empowerment and social action in a changing policy context* (Working Paper 51). Birmingham: Third Sector Research Centre.

McCabe, A., Gilchrist, A., Harris, K., Afridi, A. and Kyprianou, P. (2013) *Making the Links: Poverty, ethnicity and social networks*. Report. York: Joseph Rowntree Foundation.

McGregor, H.E. (2014) 'Exploring ethnohistory and indigenous scholarship: What is the relevance to educational historians?'. *History of Education*, 43 (4), 431–49.

Merton, R.K. (1996) 'Social structure and anomie'. In Merton, R.K. *On Social Structure and Science*. Ed. Sztompka, P. Chicago: University of Chicago Press, 132–52.

Mies, M. (1983) 'Towards a methodology for feminist research'. In Bowles, G. and Klein, R.D. (eds) *Theories of Women's Studies*. London: Routledge and Kegan Paul, 117–39.

Mirza, H.S. (1992) *Young, Female and Black*. London: Routledge.

Mirza, H.S. (ed.) (1997) *Black British Feminism: A reader*. London: Routledge.

Modood, T. (2012) *Post-Immigration 'Difference' and Integration: The case of Muslims in Western Europe: A report prepared for the British Academy* (New Paradigms in Public Policy Series). London: British Academy.

Mohanty, C.T (1997) 'Preface: Dangerous territories, territorial power, and education'. In Roman, L.G. and Eyre, L. (eds) *Dangerous Territories: Struggles for difference and equality in education*. New York: Routledge, ix–xvii.

Moosa-Mitha, M. (2005) 'Situating anti-oppressive theories within critical and difference-centred perspectives'. In Brown, L. and Strega, S. (eds) *Research as Resistance: Critical, indigenous, and anti-oppressive approaches*. Toronto: Canadian Scholars' Press, 37–72.

Nirenberg, J. (2009) 'Romani political mobilization from the first International Romani Union Congress to the European Roma, Sinti and Travellers Forum'. In Sigona, N. and Trehan, N. (eds) *Romani Politics in Contemporary Europe: Poverty, ethnic mobilization, and the neoliberal order*. Basingstoke: Palgrave Macmillan, 94–115.

Nowotny, H. (1981) 'Women in public life in Austria'. In Fuchs Epstein, C. and Laub Coser, R. (eds) *Access to Power: Cross-national studies of women and elites*. London: Allen and Unwin, 147–56.

O'Connell, J. (1996) 'Ethnicity and Irish Travellers'. In McCann, M., Ó Síocháin, S. and Ruane, J. (eds) *Irish Travellers: Culture and ethnicity*. Belfast: Institute of Irish Studies, 110–20.

Ofsted (2000) *Evaluating Educational Inclusion: Guidance for inspectors and schools* (HMI 235). London: Office for Standards in Education.

Ogbu, J.U. (1997) 'Understanding the school performance of urban Blacks: Some essential background knowledge'. In Walberg, H.J., Reyes, O. and Weissberg, R.P. (eds) *Children and Youth: Interdisciplinary Perspectives*. London: Sage, 190–222.

Okely, J. (1983) *The Traveller-Gypsies*. Cambridge: Cambridge University Press.

Okely, J. (1992) 'Anthropology and autobiography: Participatory experience and embodied knowledge'. In Okely, J. and Callaway, H. (eds) *Anthropology and Autobiography*. London: Routledge, 1–28.

Okely, J. and Callaway, H. (1992) 'Preface'. In Okely, J. and Callaway, H. (eds) *Anthropology and Autobiography*. London: Routledge, xi–xiv.

Parkin, F. (1979) *Marxism and Class Theory: A bourgeois critique*. London: Tavistock Publications.

Parry, N. (2005) 'Town's forgotten nuclear bunker'. *BBC News*, 14 December. Online. http://news.bbc.co.uk/1/hi/wales/south_west/4404340.stm (accessed 13 February 2017).

Pilkington, A. (2003) *Racial Disadvantage and Ethnic Diversity in Britain*. Basingstoke: Palgrave Macmillan.

Plowden, Lady (1967) *Children and their Primary Schools: A report of the Central Advisory Council for Education (England)*. London: HMSO.

Popple, K. (1994) 'Towards a progressive community work praxis'. In Jacobs, S. and Popple, K. (eds) *Community Work in the 1990s*. Nottingham: Spokesman, 24–36.

Posner, R.A. and Rasmusen, E.B. (1999) 'Creating and enforcing norms, with special reference to sanctions'. *International Review of Law and Economics*, 19 (3), 369–82.

Powell, R. (2011) 'Gypsy-Travellers and welfare professional discourse: On individualization and social integration'. *Antipode*, 43 (2), 471–93.

Putnam, R.D. (2000) *Bowling Alone: The collapse and revival of American community*. New York: Simon and Schuster.

Quarmby, K. (2013) *No Place to Call Home: Inside the real lives of Gypsies and Travellers*. London: Oneworld.

Reay, D. (2004) 'Gendering Bourdieu's Concept of Capitals? Emotional capital, women and social class'. In Adkins, L. and Skeggs, B. (eds) *Feminism After Bourdieu*. Oxford: Blackwell, 57–74.

Reinharz, S. (1997) 'Who Am I? The need for a variety of selves in the field'. In Hertz, R. (ed.) *Reflexivity and Voice*. Thousand Oaks, CA: Sage, 3–20.

Richardson, J. and Ryder, A. (eds) (2012) *Gypsies and Travellers: Empowerment and inclusion in British society*. Bristol: Policy Press.

Rigney, L.I. (2005) 'A first perspective of indigenous Australian participation in science: Framing indigenous research towards indigenous intellectual sovereignty'. Online. https://ncis.anu.edu.au/_lib/doc/LI_Rigney_First_perspective.pdf (accessed 7 March 2017).

Roll-Hansen, N. (2009) *Why the Distinction Between Basic (Theoretical) and Applied (Practical) Research is Important in the Politics of Science*. London: London School of Economics and Political Science, Contingency and Dissent in Science Project.

Royce, A.P. (1982) *Ethnic Identity: Strategies of diversity*. Bloomington: Indiana University Press.

Rubin, J.Z., Pruitt, D.G. and Kim, S.H. (1994) *Social Conflict: Escalation, stalemate, and settlement*. New York: McGraw-Hill.

Rüdiger, J.C.C. (1990) 'Von der Sprache und Herkunft der Zigeuner aus Indien'. In *Neuester Zuwachs der teutschen, fremden und allgemeinen Sprachkunde in eigenen Aufsätzen*, 1, 37–84. Originally 1782. Hamburg: Helmut Buske.

Runnymede Trust (2003) *Guardians of Race Equality: Perspectives on inspection and regulation*. London: Runnymede Trust.

Ryan, L., Sales, R., Tilki, M. and Siara, B. (2008) 'Social networks, social support and social capital: The experiences of recent Polish migrants in London'. *Sociology*, 42 (4), 672–90.

Ryder, A. (2014) 'Snakes and ladders: Inclusive community development and Gypsies and Travellers'. *Community Development Journal*, 49 (1), 21–36.

Ryder, A.R. (2015a) 'Gypsies and Travellers: A big or divided society?'. *Policy and Politics*, 43 (1), 101–17.

Ryder, A. (2015b) 'One Nation Conservatism: A Gypsy, Roma and Traveller case study'. *Race and Class*, 57 (2), 76–85.

Ryder, A. (2015c) *Co-producing Knowledge with Below the Radar Communities: Factionalism, commodification or partnership? A Gypsy, Roma and Traveller case study* (Discussion Paper G). Birmingham: Third Sector Research Centre.

Ryder, A. (forthcoming) 'Paradigm shift and Romani studies: Research "on" or "for" and "with" the Roma'. In Beck, S. and Ivasiuc, A. (eds) *The New Roma Activism in the New Europe*. New York: Berghahn Books.

Ryder, A. and Greenfields, M. (2010) *Roads to Success: Economic and social inclusion for Gypsies and Travellers*. Report. London: Irish Traveller Movement in Britain.

Ryder, A., Acton, T., Alexander, S., Cemlyn, S., Van Cleemput, P., Greenfields, M., Richardson, J. and Smith, D. (2011) *A Big or Divided Society? Final recommendations and report of the panel review into the Coalition Government policy on Gypsies and Travellers*. Kidwelly: Travellers Aid Trust.

Ryder, A. and Cemlyn, S. (2014) *Civil Society Monitoring on the Implementation of the National Roma Integration Strategy in the United Kingdom in 2012 and 2013*. Budapest: Decade of Roma Inclusion Secretariat Foundation.

Ryder, A., Cemlyn, S. and Acton, T. (eds) (2014) *Hearing the Voices of Gypsy, Roma and Traveller Communities: Inclusive community development*. Bristol: Policy Press.

Sande Lie, J.H. (2008) 'Post-development theory and the discourse-agency conundrum'. *Social Analysis*, 52 (3), 118–37.

Scholte, B. (1974) 'Toward a reflexive and critical anthropology'. In Hymes, D. (ed.) *Reinventing Anthropology*. New York: Vintage, 430–57

Scuzzarello, S. (2015) 'Caring multiculturalism: Power and transformation in diverse societies'. *Feminist Theory*, 16 (1), 67–86.

Sefa Dei, G.J. (2002) *Rethinking The Role of Indigenous Knowledges in the Academy* (NALL Working Paper 58). Toronto: New Approaches to Lifelong Learning.

Sen, A. (1993) 'Capability and well-being'. In Nussbaum, M. and Sen, A. (eds) *The Quality of Life*. Oxford: Clarendon Press, 30–53.

Sewell, T. (1997) *Black Masculinities and Schooling: How Black boys survive modern schooling*. Stoke-on-Trent: Trentham Books.

Shaw, M. (2008) 'Community development and the politics of community'. *Community Development Journal*, 43 (1), 24–36.

Shukra, K. (2011) 'The changing terrain of multi-culture: From anti-oppressive practice to community cohesion'. In Craig, G., Mayo, M., Popple, K., Shaw, M. and Taylor, M. (eds) *The Community Development Reader: History, themes and issues*. Bristol: Policy Press, 267–72.

Simmel, G. (1957) 'Fashion'. *American Journal of Sociology*, 62 (6), 541–58.

Smith, M. (1975) *Gypsies: Where Now?* (Young Fabian Pamphlet 42). London: Fabian Society.

Sorell, T. (1994) *Scientism: Philosophy and the infatuation with science*. London: Routledge.

Spivak, G.C. (1988) 'Can the subaltern speak?' In Nelson, C. and Grossberg, L. (eds) *Marxism and the Interpretation of Culture*. Urbana: University of Illinois Press, 271–313.

Stark, R. (1994) *Sociology*. 5th edn. Belmont, CA: Wadsworth.

Sullivan, H. (2012) 'Debate: A Big Society needs an active state'. *Policy and Politics*, 40 (1), 141–4.

Swain, J. (2005) 'Masculinities in Education'. In Kimmel, M.S., Hearn, J. and Connell, R.W. (eds) *Handbook of Studies on Men and Masculinities*. Thousand Oaks, CA: Sage, 213–229.

Swann, Lord (1985) *Education for All: The report of the Committee of Inquiry into the Education of Children from Ethnic Minority Groups* (Cmnd. 9453). London: HMSO.

Sztompka, P. (2004) 'The trauma of social change: A case of postcommunist societies'. In Alexander, J.C., Eyerman, R., Giesen, B., Smelser, N.J. and Sztompka, P. *Cultural Trauma and Collective Identity*. Berkeley: University of California Press, 155–95.

Toomey, A.H. (2011) 'Empowerment and disempowerment in community development practice: Eight roles practitioners play'. *Community Development Journal*, 46 (2), 181–95.

Traveller Movement, The (2016) *The Traveller Movement's Submission to the UN Human Rights Council's Universal Periodic Review of the UK's Human Rights Record*. London: The Traveller Movement. Online. http://travellermovement. org.uk/wp-content/uploads/TM-fully-referenced-endorsed-submission-to-the-UPR-2016-1.pdf (accessed 13 February 2017).

Tritter, J.Q. and McCallum, A. (2006) 'The snakes and ladders of user involvement: Moving beyond Arnstein'. *Health Policy*, 76 (2), 156–68.

Turner, V. (1967) *The Forest of Symbols: Aspects of Ndembu ritual*. Ithaca, NY: Cornell University Press.

Turner, V. (1995) *The Ritual Process: Structure and anti-structure*. New edn. New York: Aldine de Gruyter.

Udombana, N.J. (2000) 'The Third World and the right to development: Agenda for the next millennium'. *Human Rights Quarterly*, 22 (3), 753–87.

Vajda, V. (2015) 'Towards "critical whiteness" in Romani studies'. In *Roma Rights 2: Nothing about us without us? Roma participation in policy making and knowledge production*. Budapest: European Roma Rights Centre, 47–56.

Vanderbeck, R.M. (2009) 'Gypsy-Traveller young people and the spaces of social welfare: A critical ethnography'. *ACME: An International E-Journal for Critical Geographies*, 8 (2), 304–39.

Van Gennep, A. (2010) *The Rites of Passage*. Trans. Vizedom, M.B. and Caffee, G.L. Originally 1977. London: Routledge.

Vicari, S. (2010) 'Measuring collective action frames: A linguistic approach to frame analysis'. *Poetics: Journal of Empirical Research on Culture, the Media and the Arts*, 38 (5), 504–25.

Vijay, D. and Kulkarni, M. (2012) 'Frame changes in social movements: A case study'. *Public Management Review*, 14 (6), 747–70.

Wacquant, L. (2013) 'Bourdieu 1993: A case study in scientific consecration'. *Sociology*, 47 (1), 15–29.

Welsh, C. and Williams, R. (2005) *A Whistle-Stop Tour of Special Educational Needs*. Edinburgh: Barrington Stoke.

Widdowson, F. and Howard, A. (2008) *Disrobing the Aboriginal Industry: The deception behind Indigenous cultural preservation*. Montréal: McGill-Queen's University Press.

Williams, C.C. (2005) 'A critical evaluation of hierarchical representations of community involvement: Some lessons from the UK'. *Community Development Journal*, 40 (1), 30–8.

Willis, P. (1977) *Learning To Labor: How working class kids get working class jobs*. New York: Columbia University Press.

Willis, P., with James, S., Canaan, J. and Hurd, G. (1990) *Common Culture: Symbolic work at play in the everyday cultures of the young*. Milton Keynes: Open University Press.

Woods, P. and Hammersley, M. (1993) *Gender and Ethnicity in Schools: Ethnographic accounts*. London: Routledge in association with the Open University.

Woodward, K. (ed.) (2000) *Questioning Identity: Gender, class, nation*. London: Routledge in association with the Open University.

Woodward, K. (ed.) (2002) *Identity and Difference*. London: Sage in association with the Open University.

Wright, C., Weekes, D. and McGlaughlin, A. (2000) *'Race', Class and Gender in Exclusion from School*. London: Falmer Press.

Youdell, D. (2004) 'Identity traps or how Black students fail: The interactions between biographical, sub-cultural and learner identities'. In Ladson-Billings, G. and Gillborn, D. (eds) *The RoutledgeFalmer Reader in Multicultural Education*. London: RoutledgeFalmer, 84–102.

Zald, M.N. (1996) 'Culture, ideology, and strategic framing'. In McAdam, D., McCarthy, J.D. and Zald, M.N. (eds) *Comparative Perspectives on Social Movements: Political opportunities, mobilizing structures, and cultural framings*. Cambridge: Cambridge University Press, 261–74.

# Index

# Index